Germany's European diplomacy

MANCHESTER
UNIVERSITY PRESS

ISSUES IN GERMAN POLITICS
Edited by
Professor Charlie Jeffery, Institute for German Studies
Dr Charlie Lees, University of Sussex

Issues in German Politics is a major new series on contemporary Germany. Focusing on the post-unity era, it presents concise, scholarly analyses of the forces driving change in domestic politics and foreign policy. Key themes will be the continuing legacies of German unification and controversies surrounding Germany's role and power in Europe. The series includes contributions from political science, international relations and political economy.

Forthcoming titles include:

Hyde-Price: *Germany and European order: Enlarging NATO and the EU*

Jeffery: *The German Länder and the European Union*

Lees: *The Red–Green coalition in Germany: Politics, personalities and power*

Germany's European diplomacy
Shaping the regional milieu

Simon Bulmer
Charlie Jeffery
William E. Paterson

Manchester University Press

Copyright © Simon Bulmer, Charlie Jeffery and William E. Paterson 2000

The right of Simon Bulmer, Charlie Jeffery and William E. Paterson to be identified as the authors of this work has been asserted by them in accordance with the Copyright, Designs and Patents Act 1988.

Published by Manchester University Press
Altrincham Street, Manchester M1 7JA, UK
www.manchesteruniversitypress.co.uk

British Library Cataloguing-in-Publication Data is available

Library of Congress Cataloging-in-Publication Data is available

ISBN 978 0 7190 5855 4 paperback

First published by Manchester University Press in 2000

This edition first published 2015

The publisher has no responsibility for the persistence or accuracy of URLs for any external or third-party internet websites referred to in this book, and does not guarantee that any content on such websites is, or will remain, accurate or appropriate.

Printed by Lightning Source

Contents

	Preface	*page* vi
	Abbreviations	viii
1	Introduction: understanding Germany's European diplomacy	1
2	The institutional base for European policy-making	22
3	Relations with partners	52
4	The 1996–97 Intergovernmental Conference	76
5	Economic and Monetary Union: understanding Germany's European diplomacy	92
6	Eastern enlargement	104
7	Conclusions	124
	Select bibliography	136
	Index	144

Preface

This study is based upon the findings of research projects funded by the United Kingdom's Economic and Social Research Council (ESRC). Bulmer and Paterson's project – 'The New Germany in the New Europe' (award no. R000234004) – was researched in the period 1993–95 but has been augmented by continuing interviews and documentary research. Jeffery's project – 'Germany and the Reshaping of Europe' (award no. L213252002, 1999–2000) – is in progress, and its initial findings are reflected in particular in the sections of the book on eastern enlargement.

Our collaboration as a team of three first commenced in conjunction with a Bertelsmann Foundation/Forschungsgruppe Europa project conducted under the auspices of the Centrum für angewandte Politikwissenschaft at the Ludwig-Maximilians-Universität München. Indeed, an earlier version of the present volume was published in German, and we are grateful to Professor Werner Weidenfeld and Josef Janning for their agreeing to allow us to publish that material in revised form. Since the German volume was published, however, there have been a number of significant developments in Germany's relationship with the European Union (EU). On 1 January 1999 the Monetary Union project entered its crucial third stage. It did so without one of its principal architects, Helmut Kohl, whose Centre–Right coalition had been replaced by the Red–Green coalition of Gerhard Schröder in the Autumn of 1998. In addition, eastern enlargement had moved up the EU's agenda. The preparatory reform measures – known as Agenda 2000 – represented a central issue for the German Presidency of the EU in the first semester of 1999. This Presidency was handled under the new EU policy procedures which had been introduced by the new government. All these new developments during 1998–99 have been included in the revised version of our original study, including a new case-study chapter (Chapter 6) on EU enlargement.

In addition to thanking the ESRC for its financial support there are a number of other debts of gratitude to be expressed. We would particularly like to thank policy-making practitioners who have helped us in confidential interviews relating to the research. The Institut für Europäische Politik and the Zentrum für Europäische Integrationsforschung have offered us research facilities during visits to Germany. A number of individuals have offered direct or indirect assistance to our research and the ideas contained within the study: Jeff Anderson, Martin Burch, Gunther Hellmann, Peter Katzenstein, Josef Janning, Ludger Kühnhardt, Hanns Maull, Andreas Maurer, Michael Mentler, Patrick Meyer, Dietrich Rometsch, Otto Schmuck and Wolfgang Wessels. Thanks also to Nicola Viinikka and the team at Manchester University Press for their support. Any remaining shortcomings are, of course, our own responsibility.

We welcome discussion of the issues raised in the study. They may be directed to us at the Institute for German Studies at the University of Birmingham or the European Policy Research Unit at the University of Manchester (electronic addresses are below).

Emails simon.bulmer@man.ac.uk
c.a.jeffery@bham.ac.uk
g.u.campden@bham.ac.uk (for William Paterson)

Abbreviations

BSE	bovine spongiform encephalopathy
CAP	Common Agricultural Policy
CDU	Christian Democratic Union
CEE	Central and Eastern Europe
CFSP	Common Foreign and Security Policy
COREPER	Committee of Permanent Representatives
CSU	Christian Social Union
DBV	Deutscher Bauernverband
DM	Deutschmark
EC	European Community
ECB	European Central Bank
ECJ	European Court of Justice
ECOFIN	Council of Economics and Finance Ministers
EDC	European Defence Community
EEC	European Economic Community
EFTA	European Free Trade Association
EMS	European Monetary System
EMU	Economic and Monetary Union
EP	European Parliament
EPP	European Peoples' Party
ERM	Exchange Rate Mechanism
EU	European Union
FCC	Federal Constitutional Court
FDP	Free Democratic Party
GATT	General Agreement on Tariffs and Trade
GDP	Gross Domestic Product
IGC	Intergovernmental Conference
JHA	Justice and Home Affairs
PDS	Party of Democratic Socialism
QMV	qualified majority voting
SEA	Single European Act
SPD	Social Democratic Party
TEU	Treaty on European Union
WEU	Western European Union

1
Introduction: understanding Germany's European diplomacy

Germany and Europe: new relationship, new diplomacy?

Germany's role in Europe has been central to the entire integration project from its very outset in the Schuman Plan which launched the European Coal and Steel Community. Throughout the period of nearly forty years where the 'Monnet method' of supranational integration was conducted within the context of the Cold War (West) Germany conducted its relations in an overwhelmingly multilateralist manner. German interests were predominantly suppressed or articulated in European language. A Europeanist identity was taken on as a quasi-substitute for national identity. The Federal Republic's institutions, moreover, became interlocked with the European Communities as part of a pattern of multi-level governance evident in the domestic relationship between the federal and Länder levels.

The seismic changes brought about by the fall of the Berlin Wall in 1989, the consequent end of the Cold War, together with German unification, led to a re-opening of the German Question, at least from the perspective of some fellow Europeans. Politicians, such as Mrs Thatcher and, quite briefly, President Mitterrand, saw the new circumstances in terms of a threat arising from the Federal Republic's increased relative power within the European arena. The response of Chancellor Kohl, by contrast, was to seize the opportunity to reinforce supranational integration through a process of deepening, namely through Monetary Union and Political Union. His policy of self-restraint (*Selbsteinbindung*) came to be accepted by Mitterrand and most other European governments; it was reflected in the key reforms contained within the Maastricht Treaty on European Union (TEU).

Notwithstanding the thrust of these developments, the issue of unified

Germany's role and power in post-Cold War Europe has remained live for politicians, political scientists and economists. For economists the core concern is a rather different one from that investigated here, and concerns the continuing vitality of the German economy in a globalised context. Can the Rhineland model of capitalism compete? Is its consensual basis a hindrance to adaptation to the new competitive and technological challenges? Or does the stakeholder form of capitalism offer a less conflictual means of securing such adaptation? These issues have become even more salient with the advent of Stage III of Economic and Monetary Union (EMU), within which Germany serves as the core economy.

We recognise these as important issues. However, our concerns are with German diplomacy; with the actions of governmental elites and political parties in respect of European policy. Has the long-standing pro-integration consensus of the four decades starting in the 1950s given way to a more national-interest-focused European policy, with the removal of many of the formal external constraints that Germany confronted prior to unification in 1990? Alternatively, has there been a pattern of continuity in German diplomacy within the European Union (EU)? Of course, ours is not the first study to confront these questions.[1] Nevertheless, we believe that some critical distance is needed in order to make judgements. We argue that sufficient of the key variables have changed over the last decade to allow such judgements to be made now. What, then, have been the key changes?

- External constraints upon German sovereignty were removed as a result of the 'Two plus Four' conference, which brought together the two Germanies and the four powers (the United States (US), the Soviet Union, United Kingdom (UK) and France) to define the modalities of unification.[2] This development was not just one of liberation through the removal of constraints, for new expectations were made of Germany. The unified Germany was expected, for instance, to play a fuller, more active role in the international arena.
- The integration of the five new Länder led to the enlargement of the Federal Republic and has introduced new problems such as economic underdevelopment and environmental contamination that have found responses in the content of German European diplomacy.[3]
- The reforms of the Maastricht Treaty led the Länder governments to seek to reclaim some of the powers which they had conceded to the Federal Government as a consequence of the Europeanisation of their domestic policy responsibilities. That effort was successful and was incorporated in changes to the Basic Law.

Introduction 3

- A further, more recent domestic change has been the end of the Kohl era. The natural successor to Adenauer in his integrationist vision of European politics, Kohl was able to press ahead with supranational integration. His was a decisive role in the Maastricht Treaty. However, his replacement with a rather less committed integrationist chancellor, Gerhard Schröder, raised questions about continuity and change in German European policy.
- Within the Federal Government there have been concerns with the effectiveness of the machinery for articulating German policy in Brussels. In the academic community, options for a more effective representation of German interests came to the fore in 1998.[4] In fact, the machinery was reformed following the change of government. How far did the reforms signify or produce a change of outlook on the conduct of European diplomacy?
- Too recent to judge yet, but a variable nonetheless is the move of the seat of government to Berlin in Summer 1999. Might this move symbolise a more central-European orientation to German European policy, especially as eastern enlargement approaches? Is the Rhineland focus of integration hitherto, reinforced by its Franco–German bedrock, coming under threat?
- Finally, what has been the impact of the core component of *Selbsteinbindung*, namely EMU, on Germany's European policy?

These are major adjustments to the international context, to the character of integration itself and to domestic politics and political economy. It is for these reasons that we need to examine Germany's behaviour – its diplomacy – within the EU over the last decade. Our case studies – on the Amsterdam Treaty, Monetary Union and enlargement/Agenda 2000 – concern crucial issues for the EU and for the strategic dimension of Germany's European diplomacy. What evidence do they reveal on continuity and change? In undertaking our analysis, and in order to emphasise the long-standing special character of Germany's diplomacy, we offer some initial parallels with British diplomacy in the EU. It was suggested in October 1997 that German European policy was becoming more British in character, as the EU approached the budgetary review that was fundamental to the Agenda 2000 reforms (see Chapter 6).[5] Although these suggestions were made within Germany, they allow us (as British observers) to approach the subject of Germany's European diplomacy from an external perspective. Is German policy really becoming more 'British', more hard-nosed and calculating?

Perceptions of Germany's role in the European Union

Germany's role and diplomacy in the EU is a subject which is rarely discussed from basic principles and from a 'clean sheet'. Instead, perceptions of Germany's role are coloured by such factors as historical memory, the geographical location of the observer, and often a generational dimension as well. In consequence of these and other factors, we can see the paradoxical situation where some express concerns about Germany becoming too strong a power in the European arena, while others fear that it does not play as full a role as it should.

What are the concerns of those fearing a powerful German role in the EU? One symbolic area of concern has been with the monetary sphere: that European monetary integration has provided a basis for Germany to become powerful because of the central role of the Deutschmark (DM) in the Exchange Rate Mechanism (ERM) and, subsequently, the weight of the German economy in European EMU. This concern assumed a wider saliency in the UK because of the controversial circumstances of sterling's departure from the ERM in September 1992 and continued uncertainties over the desirability of joining EMU. More widely, latent popular concern about German power, based on historical rivalry, can periodically become inflamed, as was seen during the diplomatic crisis within the EU over British beef during 1996.[6] The controversies in late 1998 surrounding the supposed aims of Oskar Lafontaine, at that time German Finance Minister and memorably dubbed by the *Sun* as the 'most dangerous man in Europe', provide a further example.[7]

Beyond historical rivalries, German unification and the end of the Cold War prompted a new sense of relative weakness among key partners. Thus, the challenge of German unification was scarcely welcomed by Prime Minister Margaret Thatcher and some of her close political acolytes out of concern for the implications for European stability.[8] The intemperate remarks in July 1990 on the part of the then Secretary of State for Trade and Industry, Nicholas Ridley, that resulted in his resignation, gave pointed expression to this view.[9] Concerns such as these are not completely without foundation in that it would be preposterous to argue that the unified Germany is not a powerful 'player' in the integration project. Questions about the *purpose* of German power lie behind such concerns.[10] In particular, to use the well-known formula, have developments in European integration since 1990 been leading to a European Germany or to a German Europe?

At the same time, the views of other observers – or possibly the same ones! – may be coloured by rather different normative assumptions. A frustration at Germany's inability to play a more active role in the military operation during the 1991 Gulf Crisis or, prior to the Kosovo conflict in 1999, in Balkan peace-keeping has been the subject of critical comment, especially in British and American defence circles.[11] Behind this kind of criticism lies the existence of different patterns in which diplomacy is conducted, whether internationally or in the European arena. It can thus be tempting to measure German behaviour in the EU according to a set of norms of diplomacy which may not be those followed in the Federal Republic. British academic commentators have been disposed to suggesting that Germany is constrained from playing a pro-active role in the EU because of a set of largely internal constraints.[12] That it is British commentators who seem to be over-represented in this interpretation may be attributed to their use of the norms of British diplomatic behaviour as the benchmark against which to measure Germany. From a British perspective it is expected that a more centralised and activist role will be played on the global stage, reflecting what former Foreign Minister Douglas Hurd termed 'punching above one's weight'.

At the risk of exaggerating the case, then, Germany stands charged simultaneously with a dominant role in the EU as well as displaying lack of leadership. However, any attempt to present a balanced perspective on Germany's role in the EU needs to recognise the kind of normative dimension leading to such judgements if it is to offer useful insights. An evaluation that fails to take account of the institutions and norms of German political life, and focuses only on effectiveness in the projection of national interests, is likely to lack credibility and explanatory power.

In order to address this concern from the very outset, we take the view that Germany's diplomacy in the EU is not only the product of its interests, but is shaped in significant ways by its institutional arrangements and by an understanding of the kind of identity which its postwar elites have sought to project in Europe. Why must institutions and identity be brought in? We can answer this question by briefly comparing German and British views on integration purely from the perspective of interests, the normal basis of 'realist' analysis. Viewed from a British perspective, it is striking that many economic interests, especially on aspects of market integration (i.e. the internal market, budgetary policy and competition policy), are common to both member states. However, even on these matters, the two states have conducted quite different patterns of EU diplomacy. British governments of both party-political colours have pursued purposive and at times unilateral policies within the European

Community/Union. The renegotiation of the terms of British membership in 1974–75 by the Labour government of Harold Wilson and the uncompromising position of Mrs Thatcher on contributions to the European Community (EC) budget 1979–84 are variations on this theme. And this is without going into wider policy issues, such as the British opt-outs from Monetary Union and the Social Chapter or the policy of non-cooperation under John Major in the Summer of 1996 over the beef crisis. Only since the election of a Labour government under Tony Blair in 1997 has a more cooperative approach been employed in line with Blair's commitment to 'constructive engagement'.

Searching for unilateral or confrontational episodes in German European diplomacy, one is struck by the way in which the Federal Government has succeeded in avoiding isolation in Brussels, with only the question of the recognition of Slovenia and Croatia in 1991 as an exception.[13] On the budget in particular, it is striking that successive Federal Governments have not pushed their concerns about German contributions to the extent that their British counterparts have done.[14] Is it because German interests are so moderate – always in the middle-ground of negotiations – that the possibility of isolation never arises? For a large member state this seems intuitively implausible. Or is it that German institutions and the identity embedded within them result in the pursuit of policies that rarely entail isolation in EU negotiations?

Our argument in this study works from the latter presumption. We take the view that it is insufficient to analyse Germany's role in the EU without giving full attention to the institutional and identitive dimensions of that role. In some ways, this presumption is not so surprising, for it arises from one of the concerns of the occupying powers in the postwar period. They encouraged the development of a set of domestic German institutions which deconcentrated and decentralised power. Similarly, the West German state was strongly embedded in a set of international economic institutions, whether European in focus or led by the US.[15] The same position emerged, albeit with a time-lag, in respect of integration in the security and defence arenas. This situation established Germany as a 'penetrated' political system.

If one adds to this situation the need for the new West German state to gain international credibility, to secure its place in the family of democratic nations, and to live peacefully with its neighbours – at least in the West – it is little surprise that domestic institutions and a Europeanised identity came to play a key role in Germany's diplomacy. Indeed, this particular combination of factors explains the strong commitment embedded within German diplomacy to a policy of 'exaggerated multi-lateralism'.[16] These circumstances go a long way to explaining the near-absence, over the postwar period, of a discourse of 'national interests' within Germany concerning European policy, although this is not to argue that Germany has been supine in the defence of its interests. By contrast, the discourse of British European policy has been characterised by concerns with the national interest and the defence of national sovereignty, a situation promoted by the persistent divisions within both major political parties and with strong institutional and identitive dimensions.[17] Under the Schröder and Blair governments, Germany and the UK have converged somewhat from these two longer-term images of the two states' diplomacy. Nevertheless, this development does not detract from the point that narrowly defined national interests are insufficient to explain Germany's European diplomacy.

We may take this line of argument further and suggest that German diplomacy in the EU has grown to project a set of what Arnold Wolfers has termed 'milieu goals', which 'aim at shaping conditions beyond … national boundaries'.[18] Germany could not conduct a form of diplomacy based on Wolfers's other category of 'possession goals' – things held, or sought, to the 'exclusion of others' – since the circumstances which gave birth to the Bonn Republic entailed an explicit turning away from this form of power politics.

In previous instances of states pursuing milieu goals, such as British projections of a free trade policy in the nineteenth century or American postwar projections of a capitalist international economic order, there has been a notion of externalising a set of domestic institutions, interests, norms and identity onto the wider international arena.[19] We would argue that this is also true of the way in which Germany has conducted its European diplomacy, although in the early years of the integration process, policy-makers in Bonn lacked the self-confidence to do so. We argue in particular that German governments have been successful in shaping the broad structural characteristics of European integration, i.e. the regional milieu.

In making a contrast with the UK we would argue that British governments have had quite different concerns in cultivating milieu goals. A concern with securing an *arena of cooperation* within Western Europe required a change of outlook for the UK as a state which had traditionally been concerned to play continental powers off against one another in the interests of national security. While the adaptation to the political circumstances of the Cold War was conducted smoothly within the framework of NATO, the integration process has still tended to be seen by many politicians as an *arena for competition*, for supranational integration has been seen as centrally concerned with economic rather than political objectives. This outlook has tended to promote a policy of individualism within the integration project. As significant, however, has been the centralised structure of the British state, with its concentration of power in Whitehall and with its winner-takes-all parliamentary system. These characteristics – symbolised by the mythical importance ascribed to national and parliamentary sovereignty – have militated against treating European integration as a cooperative game.[20]

Germany's successful pursuit of its quite different European strategy was particularly striking under Chancellor Helmut Kohl, as we argue in Chapter 2, and was assisted by two factors. First, Kohl himself took full advantage of the institutional resources available to a chancellor to set policy guidelines, and this within a system of government which is attuned to multi-level cooperative politics. His strong personal interest in the pursuit of integration, especially in the aftermath of German unification, afforded the opportunity to play an influential role in European policy. Second, Kohl's incumbency during a period when the European integration process gained renewed momentum, starting in 1985 with the commitment to complete the Single Market, provided an opportunity to pursue milieu goals that simply was not available in the previous twenty years.

Such opportunities may not be available under Kohl's successor, Gerhard Schröder, who took over as Chancellor following the Social Democratic Party (SPD)–Green election victory in September 1998. The Schröder era is set to be a more prosaic one, partly because the leap forward at Maastricht – new pillars of policy cooperation, EMU – is now at an advanced stage of implementation and has become a matter of routine and detail. At the same time, the impending challenge of enlargement has moved beyond debates on principles, and into the detailed and largely technical negotiation of terms. Perhaps with the exception of Common Foreign and Security Policy (CFSP) in the aftermath of the Kosovo conflict, there is little scope for deploying milieu-shaping vision. In any case, Schröder represents a younger generation than Kohl for whom European integration is 'taken for granted' rather than – as Kohl described it – being a 'matter of war and peace' in Europe.[21] Thus, lacking Kohl's 'vision-thing'[22] on Europe, it hardly seems likely that Schröder will deploy the resources of his office as purposefully as Kohl did to shape such far-reaching German EU strategies.

We are in any case conscious that an over-emphasis on personality and any grand strategies of European diplomacy is a misleading basis upon which to judge Germany's role in the EU. There is also the day-to-day level of conducting policy and, at this tactical level, the very complex domestic policy-making machinery can act as a constraint upon German diplomacy in Brussels. Ministerial autonomy, coalition politics and relations with the Länder can impede the presentation of a clear policy in the day-to-day decision-making of the EU. These aspects must also form part of any assessment of Germany's power and effectiveness in the EU.

Power and effectiveness in the EU: of strategy and tactics

'Good on strategy, less good on tactics'; this might be the report on Germany as the model pupil (*Musterknabe*) of European integration. As suggested above, this study must be based on performance within both the domestic and European arenas of German EU diplomacy. So what is to be the broad line of argument in our perspective on Germany's role in the EU? Stated briefly, the argument is that integration strategy remains a matter largely for the Federal Government. Here, at the strategic level, there are relatively few veto points over the thrust of integration policy, given the prevailing party-political consensus of support for further integration. By contrast, the situation on more routine policy- and decision-making is more diffuse and much more conditional. In consequence, the *tactics* of the conduct of policy in Brussels may be much more complex. However, we argue that the influence which Germany has had over the shape of European-level institutions and policies has created a virtuous circle. The day-to-day conduct of policy is undertaken within an institutional environment with which German policy-makers are fundamentally at ease. It is rare that Germany has a policy line fundamentally at odds with its partners. Hence, any attempt to appraise German power in the EU has to appreciate the cumulative effect of its integration policy diplomacy. By virtue of being one of the major *démandeurs* of supranational solutions to domestic policy problems, the EU has been shaped into a set of institutional rules, norms and policies which are supportive of German interests. If the Federal Government is sometimes unable to advance its views on a tactical level in a wholly coherent manner, this situation is compensated for by the strategic success of German European policy which has typically brought with it a form of systemic empowerment.

The domestic level

At the domestic level what is striking is the continuation of inter-party consensus on the goal of integration, to which even the Greens have now come to subscribe, as symbolised in the appointment of Joschka Fischer to the position of Foreign Minister in the Red–Green government elected under Chancellor Gerhard Schröder in September 1998. Inter-party consensus has been important in turn for the policy pursued at elite level; the continued commitment of elites to multilateralism, to a Europeanised national identity, and to the integration project that has been facilitated by these wider circumstances. Signs of any breakdown in popular support for integration could potentially have *medium-term* ramifications for the European policies at elite level. The reference to medium-term ramifications is quite deliberate, for despite the broad domestic consensus, German integration policy has been elite-led. It has not been much more directly contingent in the short term upon public opinion. The Social Democrats' efforts in regional elections in 1996–97[23] to play upon popular concerns about the replacement of the Deutschmark, were atypical in recent times as attempts to politicise an EU issue and brought no electoral reward. Moreover, public concern at specific issues of European policy, especially where tangible costs are concerned, has in any case consistently been more conditional over the longer term.[24] However, against a backdrop of general support, such specific popular concerns – for example over budgetary contributions – have been amenable to elite 'management'. A basic level of public consensus has thus provided 'slack' which elites can exploit in order to *lead* public opinion rather than having to be mindful of, and responsive to, its day-to-day fluctuations.[25]

A continued, underlying consensus about integration is thus striking when Germany is compared to France or the UK. It provides a generally supportive backdrop for the government's diplomacy on the systemic issues relating to integration. The Single Market, the Single European Act (SEA), the Maastricht Treaty, the domestic preparation of the 1996–97 Intergovernmental Conference (IGC), the transition towards EMU and the eastern enlargement process; these have all taken place with only fleeting or minimal exceptions[26] within a broadly supportive party-political context. The broad reservoir of support, we argue, has been of great importance to giving German elites the confidence to press ahead with integrative initiatives. Under Chancellor Kohl this became an almost standard routine during the 1990s.

To be sure, Federal Governments have had to take into account the wishes of domestic actors, for example the Länder governments in the negotiation of the TEU and the Bundesbank more enduringly in establishing the framework for EMU from the TEU negotiations onwards. However, there is an alternative view to that which regards these pressures as amounting to a 'veto point' in the articulation of Bonn's negotiating strategy. Instead, they may have an enabling character. They are key features in the pursuit of milieu goals, as revealed in the processes which culminated at Maastricht in 1991 and Amsterdam in 1997. The Federal Government was able at different times to present the Länder governments, the Bundesbank and, in the light of its October 1993 judgment on the TEU, the Federal Constitutional Court (FCC) as key domestic actors whose stipulations had to be met if EU reform was to be acceptable in Germany. It is difficult for negotiating partners to quibble with Germany's domestic institutional requirements, and especially so if the institution in question is admired, as in the case of the Bundesbank. Rather than acting as domestic 'veto points' of German integration policy, these institutional features thus become part of the means whereby milieu goals are facilitated. In this way domestic institutional features are transferred to the EU level, albeit with some modification, precisely in accordance with how Wolfers defined the pursuit of milieu goals; through 'shaping conditions beyond ... national boundaries'. They contrasted strikingly with the veto points faced by John Major in his European diplomacy, where fickle public opinion and rebellious parliamentary backbenchers forced a highly obstructive policy which won little respect from EU partners, especially during the non-cooperation policy over the beef export ban and during the 1996–97 IGC. Even the Blair government, with a massive parliamentary majority, has been reluctant to lead public opinion on EMU.

In strategic terms there have been relatively few domestic 'veto points' hampering the diplomacy of German Federal Governments. With a chancellor like Helmut Kohl, who was willing and able to make use of the institutional powers available (the *Richtlinienkompetenz*), the contrast with the UK was very striking.[27] Indeed, it may be the need to moderate policy through the strong commitment to bilateral initiatives – usually with the French – that serves as a more significant constraint upon the pursuit of reform in the EU. Thus, in the 1996–97 IGC areas of Franco–German policy disagreement, such as on a stronger supranational character for the third pillar or more power for the European Parliament, were set aside but not at the cost of putting forward joint initiatives.[28] The sheer predictability of German integration policy has made Germany a trusty partner in the Franco–German relationship. Given the tradition of volatility of British policy, it is perhaps little wonder that its bilateral relations have not been of a continuing, strategic nature but have been undertaken tactically, on an issue-by-issue basis. The latter may help ensure success on individual policy decisions, but is less well attuned to shaping the goals and character of European integration more widely.

The European level
At the European level what is striking about Germany's role is that it is particularly influential in steering the direction of integration. Alone among the large founding member states it has been consistently supportive of both widening and deepening. On enlargement, it supported the 1973 enlargement, the two-stage Mediterranean enlargement (contrasting with the hesitancy of France and Italy), and the European Free Trade Association (EFTA)-enlargement of 1995. Only on Turkish membership has it remained less than enthusiastic. The historic challenge of eastward enlargement is fundamentally recognised, not least because it would entail an economic and political stabilisation for neighbours to Germany's immediate east. The potential security and economic pay-offs which arise from an open and stable East have ensured that from the early 1990s Germany has remained supportive of eastward enlargement, notwithstanding the concerns raised in particular by Schröder, but also by Kohl towards the end of his Chancellorship,[29] that the implications for German contributions to the EC budget have to be held to a reasonable level.

In respect of deepening, successive German governments have a long tradition of promoting integration: pushing ahead with the relaunch of the EC at the Hague in 1969; the move to direct elections to the European Parliament; the support for more pragmatic initiatives under Chancellor Schmidt (the creation of the European Council and of the European Monetary System (EMS)); the Genscher-Colombo Initiative which culminated under Kohl in the Stuttgart Declarations; Franco-German papers for the SEA; major inputs into the Maastricht Treaty, including the strong promotion of cooperation in Justice and Home Affairs (JHA) and the Bundesbank's role in shaping the European Central Bank Statute; and the transition to EMU from 1 January 1999.

It is this important German contribution to shaping the EU's rules which provides a firm basis to the former's power in the latter. In order to explore this aspect further, we need to consider the ways in which power can be exercised in the context of European integration.[30] Following

Lukes, and drawing on the more recent work of Guzzini,[31] we can distinguish between four conceptions of power in the EU:

1 realist power;
2 indirect institutional power;
3 unintentional power;
4 and systemic empowerment/disempowerment by the EU institutions themselves.

By *realist power* we mean traditional notions of securing one's interests in an anarchic world of international relations. Stout defence of interests, hard bargaining, the resolute defence of sovereignty; these are the characteristics of this approach. Most likely to be effective at the tactical level of European integration, e.g. over securing an abatement of budgetary contributions, it seems less likely to succeed at a strategic level within the cooperative arena of the integration project. In the latter case, it is likely to lead to either a blocking of integration or a disengagement from those aspects which do not fit national interests.

It is no coincidence that this realist kind of power seems to resemble the UK's diplomacy within the EU, given its position as a former world power, its historical diplomacy towards Europe of divide and rule, and given the centralised and adversarial nature of domestic politics which militates against the adoption of the norms of power-sharing and cooperative games within the EU. However, if the approach seems particularly characteristic of Britain's European diplomacy, that is not to argue that this approach has not been resorted to by Germany, for instance by agricultural ministers seeking to defend the interests of German farmers. That this has been done to the exasperation of other German ministries[32] as much as to other EU member states suggests, though, that this has more to do with the institutional pluralism than realist power projection.

A more subtle way of securing a powerful position in the EU can come from the articulation of *indirect institutional power*. Here the concern is explicitly with shaping the EU's rules. We have already set out instances of German governments seeking to shape the integration process through institutional, constitutional or major policy initiatives (deepening) or through enlargement. Moreover, as already argued, a state which is successful in its strong pursuit of supranational solutions to domestic problems is likely to have a disproportionately large impact upon the character of supranational governance. It is through indirect institutional power, then, that Germany has been able to project its milieu goals. As already noted, Germany has been assisted by a relatively favourable set of domestic political circumstances: the positions of the main parties and of public opinion. It has also been assisted by a domestic political system which is used to multi-level governance and the norms of consensus-building. Thus, Federal Governments typically possess a promising basis on which to secure their milieu goals.

For example, in the Maastricht negotiations Germany's advocacy of the development of JHA cooperation bore fruit, and was consolidated to some extent in the Amsterdam Treaty. More strikingly, Chancellor Kohl was also prepared at Maastricht to override a rationalist policy on monetary integration – which would have been the continuance of the EMS – by using the political override of seeking to bind Germany into the supranational system. Pure rationalism would have suggested that a kind of DM-zone had already been created, that it provided a zone of trading stability for Germany, and that it entailed far fewer risks than the relative unknown of EMU. This narrower, economic view was overridden. Separately, the prestige of negotiators from the Bundesbank facilitated the creation of a European Central Bank Statute which bore strong resemblance to the Frankfurt model, and which formed the basis on which EMU was launched in 1999.[33]

For comparative purposes, since one needs comparison to illustrate Germany's distinctiveness, it is striking that British governments have been much less successful at projecting indirect institutional power. Why? First, there has been a reluctance to play the 'cooperative game' at the level of abstract political principles. British politicians are unclear what the political goals of integration are, and are reluctant to support European integration as an abstract enterprise rather than on specific pragmatic grounds. British politicians are prone to dismiss German politicians' abstract pronouncements in favour of integration as mere rhetoric. In fact, these pronouncements are reflective of deeply embedded norms that are constitutive of Germany's identity. Moreover, supranational constitutional engineering is regarded with particular suspicion. Second, each of the two main parties has been divided internally over European matters, so it has only been at times when the government has had a commanding majority in the House of Commons that a more constructive diplomacy has been possible; witness the ability to ratify the SEA without significant opposition in the Thatcher era, and the more cooperative policies pursued under Prime Minister Blair since 1997. A third explanation might derive from the different character of British institutions: the absence until the Blair government of an explicit constitutionalism; a majoritarian parliamentary system; a tradition of common law; and the absence of a consensualism which is rooted in many continental institutional systems and is an expression of different catholic/christian traditions.[34]

Unintentional power needs also to be taken into account. What is meant by this terminology is the kind of situation where power is exerted but not as the result of diplomacy. For a state such as Germany, which is the largest economic power in the EU and has had the strongest national currency in Europe, the scope for the exercise of unintentional power is great. The very deconcentration and decentralisation of authority within Germany can also be a contributory factor. Perhaps the prime example of the exercise of such power was seen in the EMS in the period after German unification.[35] The Bundesbank followed its script of safeguarding the stability of the DM and restraining any inflationary pressure emerging from the increased borrowing associated with unification and the overhauling of the economic infrastructure of the five new Länder. Due to the DM's anchor role in the ERM the higher interest rates had also to be endured in neighbouring states, including France. This was so despite the fact that the economic fundamentals in the other states were quite different. The logic of their suffering higher interest rates stemmed from the structure of the ERM and from the script-driven policies of the Bundesbank. Earlier decisions about the operation of the ERM, such as the Basle–Nyborg Agreement and the commitment to moving further to EMU, had created a monetary regime in which realignments were frowned upon at a time when they might have assisted other states from suffering the costs in higher unemployment of the higher interest rates. This situation, therefore, was a product of a new set of norms in the ERM, i.e. of resisting realignments, and of the Bundesbank pursuing its domestic policy role. Considering the international repercussions of domestic monetary policy was not a function of the autonomous Bundesbank. The deconcentration of executive power in Germany facilitated a distinction between a 'Frankfurt European policy' characterised more by (the unintentional) pursuit of national interests than the European policy of Bonn.

Hence the asymmetrical shock of unification to the German economy had a strong impact on fellow members in the ERM, and was a contributory factor to the exit of the Italian lira and the pound sterling from the system in 1992. This episode illustrates the way in which development of the German economy, as the powerhouse of the European economy, has an important influence within the EU. However, there was no deliberate pursuit of policy in order to achieve these ends. Rather the impact on other member states was the accidental consequence of German dispositional power. In addition, unintentional power has an important impact on perceptions of Germany's role in Europe; it certainly confirmed the predispositions of those Euro-sceptics in the UK who were dubious about the purposes of German policy.[36]

In an interdependent EU, a crisis in any member state may have an impact elsewhere; such repercussions are not just the result of *German* unintentional power. One only needs to look at the consequences of scientific opinion on the possible transmission of bovine spongiform encephalopathy (BSE) to humans to see how a disease largely confined to the UK beef industry had repercussions over a period of years for the entire European beef market. However, it is clear that the economic centrality of Germany in the EU gives it dispositional power which can have an impact on the core macro-economic policies of the other member states. This is unlikely to disappear in EMU; the sheer weight of the German economy will remain a constant point of reference in European economic decision-making. The UK cannot match this centrality and, the BSE crisis notwithstanding, is less likely to be associated with the unintentional exercise of power. Indeed, to the extent that the UK remains outside EU policies like EMU or parts of the Amsterdam Treaty provisions on home affairs, then the scope for this to happen is reduced.

Finally, there is the case of *systemic empowerment* (or, indeed, disempowerment) by the EU institutions themselves. All institutions entail some mobilisation of bias. The EU is no exception to this rule. Does the disposition of the EU institutions serve Germany well or badly? Here we would argue that there is a kind of payback from Germany's extensive use of indirect institutional power. As a major *démandeur* of EU solutions to domestic problems – from the combating of cross-border crime to the management of environmental problems – Germany has tended to shape the policy profile of the *EU in a way that suits its ends*.[37] Moreover, the supply of institutional and policy models from German experience – as illustrated in the context of the TEU in Chapter 2 – creates a supranational set of institutions that are similar to those at the domestic level. Cumulatively, this creates a policy-making environment which is congenial to German negotiators.[38] Acquainted with the operation of a similar institutional system at home, German negotiators are able to use this familiarity to make up for any of their shortcomings on the tactical level of policy-making arising from the need to consult a large number of institutional actors to agree a German negotiating position. It is a difficult point to prove but might it be this systemic empowerment which helps explain why Germany is rarely isolated in EU negotiations? For the UK, the aforementioned difficulties in shaping the EU rules through indirect institutional power mean that the opportunity to receive systemic empowerment as a kind of payback is largely absent. That this has been so was demonstrated most graphically by the problems the UK encountered when it joined the EC in 1973. It had to accept the existing *acquis communautaire*. The poor match between British interests and the pre-established rules governing the Common Agricultural Policy (CAP) and the EC budget led to protracted negotiations designed to reform supranational rules. To the extent that the UK fails to participate in various examples of differentiated integration, but elects to join later, it will not benefit from the kind of systemic empowerment enjoyed by Germany.

To conclude this introduction, we argue that Germany's strategic diplomacy, despite a rather more mixed performance at the tactical level owing to institutional fragmentation, has been successful in developing its milieu goals within the EU. In so doing, it has had an important impact upon the shape of the institutions, policies and broad values of the EU. Contrasts with circumstances in the UK have been designed to highlight the distinctive nature of German diplomacy, with its great emphasis upon indirect institutional power. A more British style of European policy would imply for German diplomacy a shift towards projecting a more realist form of power within the EU.

In the following chapters we explore the distinctiveness of German diplomacy by addressing some of the specific components of domestic European policy-making. In particular, have these characteristics persisted? Chapter 2 deals with the configuration of domestic institutions involved in European policy-making, dealing in turn with the Federal Government, the role played by political parties and the Länder. Separate attention is given to the ways in which forms of 'institutional export' have impacted on the virtuous circle of indirect institutional power and systemic empowerment. Chapter 3 examines aspects of alliance-building at the level of the member states, demonstrating ways in which the Europeanised identity Germany seeks to project may support – or impede – positive relations with EU partners in the development of the Union.

Chapters 4 to 6 meld the two dimensions of internal institutional factors and external alliance-building capability in a series of case studies. These deal in turn with German European diplomacy in the 1996–97 IGC, in the preparations for EMU through to its launch in 1999, and in the protracted debates on EU eastward enlargement which accelerated from

1997 with the Agenda 2000 package of pre-enlargement policy and budgetary reform and the opening of formal accession negotiation with five Eastern candidates in 1998. The choice of cases is designed to capture the main issues which have dominated the EU's agenda in the second half of the 1990s and thus to deliver a balanced, comparative perspective on the character of German EU diplomacy across a range of issue areas. It is also designed to capture questions of change raised by the transition from Kohl to Schröder. The IGC and EMU in particular were unambiguously Kohl's projects; but while Kohl invested considerable energy in securing wider acceptance of the enlargement project, the key decisions on the concrete terms of enlargement will be taken under Schröder. Does this make a difference? There are certainly identifiable indices of change: the generational shift from visionary elder statesman to a younger, more pragmatic politician less bound up, for example, in the historical resonances of the relationship with France, and a new balance of institutional factors shaped both by new personalities, but also by a reconfiguration of departmental responsibilities in European policy. Are these changes set to alter the purpose of German power in the EU? The issue of German power, and wider questions of evaluation of how Germany has shaped its regional milieu since 1990, will be addressed in our Conclusions in Chapter 7.

Notes

1 See, for instance, C. Lankowski (ed.), *Germany and the European Community: Beyond Hegemony and Containment?* (London: Macmillan; New York: St Martin's, 1992); P. Katzenstein (ed.), *Tamed Power: Germany in Europe* (Ithaca, NY: Cornell University Press, 1997).
2 See P. Zelikow and C. Rice, *Germany Unified and Europe Transformed* (Cambridge, MA: Harvard University Press, 1995), Ch. 5.
3 See J. Anderson, *German Unification and the Union of Europe: The Domestic Politics of Integration Policy* (Cambridge: Cambridge University Press, 1999).
4 As reflected in the sub-title of W. Weidenfeld (ed.), *Deutsche Europapolitik: Optionen wirksamer Interessenvertretung* (Bonn: Europa Union Verlag, 1998); see especially the chapter by Janning and Meyer.
5 Source P. Hort, 'Die deutsche Europa-Politik wird "britischer". Bonn stellt das Integrationsmodell in Frage und orientiert sich mehr an Kosten und Nutzen', in *Franfurter Allgemeiner Zeitung*, 30 October 1997, 16.
6 See M. Westlake, 'Keynote Article: "Mad Cows and Englishmen" – The International Consequences of the BSE Crisis', *The European Union 1996: Annual Review of Activities, Journal of Common Market Studies*, 35 (special issue) (1997), 11–36.
7 *Sun*, 25 November 1998, 2 December 1998.

8 See, for instance, P. Zelikow and C. Rice, *Germany Unified and Europe Transformed* (Cambridge, MA: Harvard University Press, 1995); M. Thatcher, *The Downing Street Years* (London: Harper Collins, 1993), 790–1, 813–15; K. Diekmann and R. Reuth, *Helmut Kohl: Ich wollte Deutschlands Einheit* (Berlin: Propyläen, 1996), 340–3.
9 As reported in the *Spectator*, 14 July 1990.
10 See A-M. Le Gloannec, 'The Purpose of German Power', in Z. Laïki (ed.), *Power and Purpose after the Cold War* (Providence: Berg Publishers).
11 Cf. D. Conversi, 'German-Bashing and the Breakup of Yugoslavia', *The Donald W. Treadgold Papers in Russian, East European and Central Asian Studies*, No. 16, University of Washington (1998).
12 E.g. S. Bulmer and W. Paterson, 'European Policy-Making in the Federal Republic: Internal and External Limits to Leadership', in W. Wessels and E. Regelsberger (eds), *The Federal Republic of Germany and the European Community: The Presidency and Beyond* (Bonn: Europa Union Verlag, 1987); C. Jeffery, 'A Giant with Feet of Clay? United Germany in the European Union', *University of Birmingham Discussion Papers in German Studies*, No. IGS95/6 (1995). The external limits on Germany referred to in earlier publications were reduced by the end of the Cold War and German unification. See W. Paterson, 'Beyond Semi-Sovereignty: The New Germany in the New Europe', *German Politics*, 5 (1996).
13 We deliberately set aside at this point issues of the implementation of EC law or of the interaction between the European and German legal systems. On the recognition of Slovenia and Croatia, see J. Anderson and J. Goodman, 'Mars or Minerva? A United Germany in a Post-Cold War Europe', in R. O. Keohane, J. S. Nye and S. Hoffmann (eds), *After the Cold War: International Institutions and State Strategies in Europe, 1989–1991* (Cambridge, MA: Harvard University Press, 1993); also B. Crawford, 'German Foreign Policy and European Political Cooperation: The Diplomatic Recognition of Croatia in 1991', *German Politics and Society*, 13, Summer (1995), and Conversi, 'German-Bashing and the Breakup of Yugoslavia'.
14 Despite more robust rhetoric in the Agenda 2000 reform debate, the Schröder government secured only modest concessions in the eventual agreement reached at the March 1999 European Council in Berlin (see Ch. 6 for a more detailed discussion).
15 M. Kreile, 'West Germany: The Dynamics of Expansion', in P. Katzenstein (ed.), *Between Power and Plenty: Foreign Economic Policies of Advanced Industrial States* (Madison: University of Wisconsin Press, 1978).
16 The term is used by J. Anderson, 'Hard Interests, Soft Power, and Germany's Changing Role in Europe', in P. Katzenstein (ed.), *Tamed Power: Germany in Europe* (Ithaca, NY: Cornell University Press, 1997), 85.
17 On the role of institutions and their norms in the formulation of British European policy, see K. Armstrong and S. Bulmer, 'The United Kingdom', in D. Rometsch and W. Wessels (eds), *The European Union and Member States:*

Towards Institutional Fusion? (Manchester: Manchester University Press, 1996).

18 A. Wolfers, *Discord and Collaboration* (Baltimore: Johns Hopkins, 1962), 72–5.

19 On the American case, see C. Maier, 'The Politics of Productivity: Foundations of American International Economic Policy After World War II', in Katzenstein, *Between Power and Plenty*. See also A-M. Burley, 'Regulating the World: Multilateralism, International Law and the Projection of the New Deal Regulatory State', in J. G. Ruggie (ed.), *Multilateralism Matters: The Theory and Praxis of an Institutional Form* (New York: Columbia University Press, 1993).

20 Paranthetically we should note that the Blair government's constitutional reform project in the UK is likely to trigger subtle changes in the UK's European diplomacy: see K. Armstrong and S. Bulmer, 'The United Kingdom: Between Political Controversy and Administrative Efficiency', in W. Wessels, A. Maurer and J. Mittag (eds), *Fifteen into One? The European Union and its Member States* (Manchester: Manchester University Press, 2000).

21 The contrast was articulated by Schröder himself in an interview with *Der Spiegel*, 4 January 1999, 42.

22 W. Paterson, 'Helmut Kohl, "The Vision Thing" and Escaping the Semi-Sovereignty Trap', in C. Clemens and W. E. Paterson (eds), *The Kohl Chancellorship* (London: Frank Cass, 1998).

23 See further in Ch. 5.

24 See for instance the argument presented in S. Bulmer and W. Paterson, *The Federal Republic of Germany and the European Community* (London: Allen & Unwin, 1987), Ch. 5.

25 This 'slack' and the financial resources to contribute to the EC budget were, however, rather less in evidence in Germany in the context of the Agenda 2000 debates which culminated in early 1999 (see Ch. 6). In consequence, there is a question mark against a continuing autonomy for political elites from public opinion.

26 E.g. the flirtation with EMU-scepticism by the SPD in 1996–97 and the clear difference between the CDU and SPD on the need to reform the CAP as a precondition for EU enlargement. See further in Chs 5 and 6.

27 The relative absence of veto points is particularly striking when European policy is compared with domestic economic policy. The complexity of negotiations with the Länder governments on issues such as tax reform make this contrast all too apparent.

28 In his statement on European policy and the IGC to the Bundestag on 10 October 1996, Foreign Minister Kinkel underlined that 'it is virtually expected that we take the lead with the French'. He was referring to a planned joint initiative for the Dublin European Council in December. See 'Erklärung der Bundesregierung zur Europapolitik, insbesondere zum Stand der Regierungskonferenz', in *Bulletin*, Nr. 81, 870, 15 October 1996. In fact, only a

Introduction 21

week later an important joint initiative was launched, aimed to enable those states wishing to integrate more rapidly to be able to do so. The initiative centred on the incorporation of flexibility clauses into the existing treaties: see 'Verstärkte Zusammenarbeit im Hinblick auf die weitere Vertiefung des europäischen Einigungswerks. Gemeinsamer deutsch–französischer Diskussionsbeitrag für die Regierungskonferenz', Bonn, 17 October 1996. See further in Ch. 4.

29 See further in Ch. 6.
30 This theme is pursued in more detail in S. Bulmer, 'Shaping the Rules? The Constitutive Politics of the European Union and German Power', in Katzenstein, *Tamed Power: Germany in Europe*, 49–79.
31 S. Lukes, *Power: A Radical View* (London: Macmillan, 1974); S. Guzzini, 'Structural Power: The Limits of Neorealist Power Analysis', *International Organisation*, 47 (Summer 1993).
32 See Bulmer and Paterson, *The Federal Republic of Germany and the European Community*, 67–77.
33 See K. Dyson, *Elusive Union: The Process of Economic and Monetary Union in Europe* (Harlow: Longman, 1994), 154–9. See also the discussion in Ch. 2 on 'institutional export'.
34 Though this is arguably being ameliorated by the programme of constitutional reforms launched by the Blair government which, following Neal Ascherson, is 'deeply influenced by Europe, by the "rights culture" and consensus politics and decentralised government of the states which make up the European Union', and which may in due course modify the UK's terms of engagement with its European partners. See Neal Ascherson, 'Measure by Measure, Blair Plans the Polite Revolution', *Independent on Sunday*, 4 May 1997, and W. Paterson and C. Jeffery, *Großbritannien nach dem Machtwechsel: New Labour, Devolution und Europapolitik* (St. Augustin: Konrad-Adenauer-Stiftung Arbeitspapiere, 1997), 33–4.
35 This example is also used by Guzzini in his 'Structural Power: The Limits of Neorealist Analysis'.
36 Cf. J. Buller and C. Jeffery, 'Britain, Germany and the Deepening of Europe', in K. Larres and E. Meehan (eds), *Uneasy Allies: British–German Relations and European Integration Since 1945* (Oxford: Oxford University Press, 2000).
37 On German influence on the character of EU environmental policy see A. Sbragia, 'Environmental Policy: The "Push–Pull" of Policy-Making', in H. Wallace and W. Wallace (eds), *Policy-Making in the European Union*, 3rd edn (Oxford: Oxford University Press, 1996).
38 For more on the congruence of the institutions, policies and their norms of the EU with their counterparts in Germany, see Bulmer, 'Shaping the Rules?'

2
The institutional base for European policy-making

The domestic institutional base for European policy-making in the Federal Republic is without doubt the most deconcentrated in the EU. The constitutional bases of German government purposefully disperse policy-making powers along two axes: a horizontal axis at the level of the Federal Government, which allows individual ministries to pursue their own 'house' policies, and a vertical axis along which decision-making powers are divided and/or shared between federal-level institutions and those of the Länder. As the European integration process has developed and, in the last ten to fifteen years in particular, has increasingly perforated the domestic decision-making arena, this constitutional dispersal of power has been progressively externalised in Germany's European diplomacy. Additional roles in European policy have also – with varying degrees of success – been claimed by other domestic actors, notably the Bundesbank, the major political parties and the FCC, consolidating the dispersed and deconcentrated character of European policy-making. The process and features of the externalisation of internal structures of government are examined below under headings dealing in turn with the Federal Government, the political parties, the Länder and the wider question of institutional 'export'.

Policy-making in the Federal Government

The Federal Government's machinery for making European policy takes its cues from Article 65 of the Basic Law. The Chancellor has the competence to set the guidelines of policy but individual ministries conduct policy in their own spheres in relative autonomy. The role of the Cabinet is limited, confined to preparations of European Council meetings or resolving inter-ministerial disputes over the substance of European policy. As we suggested in Chapter 1, Chancellor Kohl chose to utilise his *Richtlinienkompetenz* very fully during the 1990s. A number of factors conspired to allow him to do this. First, all Chancellors have a selective interest and in the case of Kohl, *Europapolitik* was probably his strongest such interest. Moreover, his handling of the German unity process greatly strengthened his reputation and capacity for influence both inside and outside Germany. This period was also accompanied by a strengthening of the capacity of the Chancellor's Office in coordinating the strategic priorities of European policy alongside the existing coordinating roles played by the Foreign Office and the Economics Ministry (see p. 24).[1] Kohl was also aided in exercising his *Richtlinienkompetenz* by external actors looking to him for leadership. In particular, the continued stress on the Franco–German relationship (see Chapter 3) was a structural 'given' that privileged the role of the Chancellor as the interlocutor of the French President.[2] Rarely was a forthcoming EU Summit not prefigured by a joint Franco–German policy statement arising from a Franco–German bilateral.

The strategic importance of the European Council in the governance system of the EU also facilitated chancellorial intervention, at the same time boosting the claims of the Chancellor's Office to the coordination of strategic priority-setting for the Federal Government. Moreover, the pursuit of milieu goals was reflected in an agenda which was dominated by the kind of institutional issues which tend to privilege chancellorial intervention. This situation has proved to be most marked during IGCs and in the negotiations on EMU. While Chancellors have often played such a role in institutional integration issues, the degree of dominance enjoyed by Kohl reflected his experience, success, external standing and a selective interest in European integration without parallel since Adenauer.

The 'fit' between the *Richtlinienkompetenz* and a policy stance which accorded a central place to milieu goals had additional implications. Such goals have, by definition, a tendency to be overarching, far-reaching and transformatory in character, and therefore – unlike the technical policy preserves of individual, specialist ministers – require legitimation by the head of government. It was also easier for Kohl to pursue a strategic vision by reference to the *Richtlinienkompetenz* in European policy than in domestic issues since European policy – with the exception of agriculture – is typically much more autonomous of domestic interests. Kohl could therefore exploit the multi-levelled character of much of European policy to stamp his own *Handschrift* on the policy process. His long incumbency also contributed to the realisation of strategic, milieu goals since strategic issues by definition, and unlike tactical issues, are necessarily long term.

It is unlikely that this confluence of historical, personal and institutional factors which facilitated Kohl's EU policy role in the 1990s will easily be repeated. Few successors will have the benefit of the accumulated political weight which comes from such a long tenure. And his immediate successor, Gerhard Schröder, has (perhaps understandably) yet to set out longer-term strategic goals, preferring instead to throw the authority of his office into narrower and more short-term concerns, in particular to hold in check the German contribution to the EU budget. He has also favoured a less exclusive alliance strategy, opening up other partnership opportunities alongside the Franco–German tandem which has traditionally driven forward the major, strategic initiatives in European integration. Finally, on establishing his government towards the end of 1998, the administrative machinery for European policy-making was reshaped,[3] arguably making it less amenable to purposeful strategic coordination.

The net result is an administration focused less on the long term and the strategic and more on near-term questions of detail and tactics. On such questions, the role of the Chancellor has always been much less pronounced and the coordination of policy rather less effective. Symbolically, there have been *two* separate focal points of policy coordination: the European Division of the Foreign Office, established only in 1993, and Division E of the Federal Ministry of Economics, which held the portfolio for coordination from the creation of the European Coal and Steel Community through to the changes introduced by the Schröder government in 1998. The division of labour between Foreign Office and Economics Ministry was never entirely clear-cut, though the Foreign Office broadly dealt with European foreign policy (European Political Cooperation and subsequently the CFSP) and longer-term political priorities of integration policy (though the Chancellor's Office increasingly emerged as a competitor here). The Economics Ministry broadly focused on economic questions of integration, while also acting as 'post-box' for the distribution of EU policy documentation to the other ministries, the Bundestag and the Bundesrat, and as communication channel with the Permanent Representation in Brussels.

The 1998 reform entailed the transfer of the Economics Ministry's European division to the Finance Ministry. This added the Economics Ministry's post-box function and some of its Brussels liaison functions to existing Finance Ministry responsibilities concerning EMU and the EU budget. The Economics Ministry was left only with responsibility for the

EU dimension of activities within its functional domain, such as the internal market or trade policy. At the same time, the Foreign Office secured a small increase in its powers. Having gradually encroached on the Economics Ministry's once exclusive right to issue instructions to the German Permanent Representation (e.g. on IGCs and eastern enlargement), it had this role formalised and upgraded in a formal division of labour agreed with the Finance Ministry at the end of 1998. In addition, it is the only ministry with coordinating functions across all three pillars of the EU (though, of course, the Chancellor's Office may still intervene).

What is the effect of this complex coordination structure? The existence of multiple coordination responsibilities always held before 1998 the potential for both ambiguities and turf battles to develop in the coordination process and therefore to leave an unusually broad leeway for individual ministries to pursue sectorised 'house' policies not necessarily formally adopted as policies of the Federal Government as a whole (see pp. 26–7). This situation does not seem set to change with the new arrangements introduced in 1998. The Foreign Office has expanded its authority both functionally and politically – the latter via Joschka Fischer's highly regarded leadership skills. This pattern would tend to privilege a wider, more strategic view of German priorities, rooted in what was essentially the founding rationale of the Foreign Office in placing Germany at the heart of a multilateralising Europe. However, the quality of the interactions it will have with the Finance Ministry remains unclear. The latter certainly lost in political authority after the resignation of Oskar Lafontaine, but retains both a functional pedigree as one of the great offices of state and a very different rationale. This is, naturally enough, money-focused and privileges a narrower, even zero-sum conception of German priorities; the contrast with the positive-sum conceptions of both Economics Ministry (with its free-trade rationale) and the multilateralising Foreign Office is striking. Finance Ministry officials regard the shift from Economics to Finance as supporting a shift towards a more 'streamlined', 'cost-conscious' and 'realistic' approach to EU policy-making.[4]

The clashing rationales of the two coordinating ministries do not seem set to offer clear leadership. Equally, therefore, a strong sectorisation of European policy seems set to continue in particular on routine policy matters; while all ministries are affected by the EU to some extent, there is no single and unambiguously authoritative 'ringmaster' to oversee coherence. The tendency to sectorisation can, moreover, be reinforced by the dynamics of coalition politics, which may strengthen different, sectoral policy positions across different ministries, and by the political character of the upper echelons of the German civil service, which further strengthens allegiance to political patrons rather than to the civil service as a whole. The coalition dynamic was strongly evident during the Kohl era in the persistent differences of departmental and party-political/ ideological perspective between a liberal, free trade-orientated Economics Ministry headed by the Free Democratic Party (FDP) and a protectionist Agriculture Ministry headed by ministers from either the Christian Democratic Union (CDU) or its Bavarian sister party the Christian Social Union (CSU); both the latter are closely linked with the farmers union, the Deutscher Bauernverband (DBV). The influence of coalition politics on European policy reappeared surprisingly quickly under Schröder in the embarrassingly public difference of opinion between the Green Environment Minister Jürgen Trittin and Chancellor Schröder on a draft EU directive on the recycling of cars at the end of their useful lives; ultimately Schröder's close links with the car industry won the day, but not without exposing his government's internal differences via Trittin's painfully public recantation in the Council of Environmental Ministers.[5]

The phenomenon of sectorisation has become all the more significant in proportion to the steady extension of EU competence since the mid-1980s. More ministries are now more extensively and more regularly engaged with European policy matters than fifteen years ago. The traditional Euro-ministries – the Foreign Office, Economics and Agriculture – have been joined by a number of others with intensive European policy interests and responsibilities since the SEA and the TEU, in particular Finance (in regard to EMU and in close liaison with the Bundesbank), Interior and Justice (both with extensive concerns in the EU third pillar of Justice and Home Affairs Cooperation) and Environment. Examples of sectorisation are numerous. Although the Federal Ministry for Food, Agriculture and Forestry, traditionally a bastion of sectorisation, has reluctantly come to recognise the merits of reform of the CAP, it still retains a protective outlook towards its domestic farming community. It was striking during the negotiation of the General Agreement on Tariffs and Trade (GATT) Uruguay Round that there was uncertainty over whether to side with other protective agriculture ministers, notably in France, or to recognise the much wider issues of trade policy at stake for the German economy as a whole. Ultimately the latter view prevailed, as it is likely to do on similar issues under the Schröder government. An SPD–Green administration naturally lacks the party-political closeness (and electoral indebtedness) to the farming lobby of a government led by the CDU/CSU. The political weight of the Agriculture Ministry has fallen since 1998 accordingly.

In the aftermath of German unification, the Economics Ministry has found itself seeking to retain its ordo-liberal principles, while seeking exceptional treatment for the specific economic problems of the five new Länder. The enunciation of liberal economic principles at a time when Germany is the largest provider of subsidies to its industries within the EU is less than convincing, as was the apparent inability to 'bring to order' the government of Saxony, when the latter had been asked by the European Commission to repay subsidies given for the establishment of a new Volkswagen plant.[6] Beyond Bonn, the Bundesbank's responsibility for monetary policy, arising from its statutory duties and formal independence from the Federal Government, led on occasion (pre-EMU) to German positions on the EU's Monetary Committee appearing somewhat uncoordinated, with the Bundesbank and the Finance Ministry putting forward inconsistent positions.[7] The perception was that of a separate, more hawkish European policy being conducted in Frankfurt.[8] A similar syndrome has emerged with the more prominent role the Interior Ministry has come to take in third pillar and eastern enlargement matters (the free movement of labour in particular); Interior Ministry representatives are said both to exaggerate the scope of concerns in their field beyond that identified by other German ministries, and to pursue them in Brussels rather more brusquely than is normal.[9]

What are the consequences of this sectorised policy? Policy becomes clear only at a late stage, meaning that it may not be influential in the Commission's thinking. This outcome is particularly likely on major, cross-departmental policy that has not engaged the interest of the Chancellor. Where one ministry clearly has the lead, it may be more influential, as the Agriculture Ministry has been over the years. However, there then arises the question of whether the policy pursued is that of the Federal Government or of the ministry concerned. For many years the Agriculture Ministry appeared to pursue a high-cost policy of support for German farmers while the Finance Ministry was seeking to constrain EC expenditure. An equivalent picture may be emerging under Schröder of an interventionist Environment Ministry pitched against a deregulationist Chancellor's Office and Economics Ministry.[10]

The Federal Government's weak coordination militates against the use of the Brussels networks of lobbying, such as of Commission *cabinets*. Poor coordination also hampers the pursuit of a personnel policy in the Commission designed to ensure that senior positions in the Directorates-

General are occupied by sympathetic officials. Consequently, the Permanent Representation cannot promote German policy in the more direct way that its French and British counterparts can. Overall, the mind-set and institutional arrangements of the European policy-makers in the Federal Government are simply not attuned to the most effective representation of governmental policy.

To summarise: the sectorisation of German policy is part of a long-standing tradition. It owes its origins to strong departmental norms. They, in turn, are amplified by coalition politics, which encourages the formation of political fiefdoms. The phenomenon of sectorisation can make the substance of Bonn/Berlin's policy difficult for EU partners – most of which have more centralised patterns of policy management – to be sure of. Officials in Britain are known, for example, to have to resort to telephoning different German federal ministries and officials in order to make a judgement on what policy line will eventually be adopted by German negotiators in the Committee of Permanent Representatives (COREPER) and the Council. The British Embassy in Germany may even be involved in trying to assess what the final German policy line will be. The reconciliation of German positions may occur only at a late stage in negotiations – to the irritation of partners. It is circumstances such as these which contribute to a less effective German articulation of policy on the tactical rather than the strategic level. This is recognised within the Federal Government; several interview partners in the federal ministries have expressed unsolicited admiration for the efficiency of British preparations (if not always the substance of British policy) for EU negotiations.[11] The syndrome of sectoral conflict, weak coordination and the arrival at a German position only at a late stage in negotiation does, however, bring one benefit: the likely avoidance of isolation and the last-minute achievement of trade-offs which are less open to those members like the UK which *enter* negotiations with a clear and well-coordinated set of priorities that may entail less flexibility.

Political parties and Europe

Beyond the contribution they make to policy sectorisation in the framework of coalition politics, Germany's parties have a much broader scope of engagement in European policy debates. Since the latter part of the 1950s, this has typically been conducted with a high degree of consensus about the purposes and goals of European integration (which has now been consolidated by the transformation of the Greens into a pro-integration force). Unusually in international comparison, this positive engagement is conducted not only in the domestic arena, but is also purposefully mobilised externally in a range of activities directed at opinion-shaping beyond Germany. The domestic and external arenas of party-political Euro-engagement are discussed in turn in the following.

Internal pressures
The internal domestic party-political consensus on Europe is a very important facilitator of the long-term strategic strength of German European policy. Freed from the constant turbulence and very restricted margin of autonomy that Europe's divisiveness as an issue imposes on the governments of the UK, German Federal Governments are able to look at the question of German interests in the long term rather than extracting the maximum leverage on a case-by-case basis.[12]

However, while there has been an overall party consensus on European policy, there are differences of emphasis. Coalition politics conducted in the context of the sectoral policies identified with individual ministries can interact to make these differences important. The greatest potential for the impact of party differences occurs at the creation of a new government since the coalition agreements are negotiated and signed by party chairmen. In November 1994 this meant that the CSU was represented by Theo Waigel, a factor which served to minimise any party reservations on EMU on the relevant section of the coalition agreement since he was in any case Finance Minister. The FDP had a much more obvious impact on the agreement and used the negotiation to contain the 'hard core' policy promulgated by the CDU/CSU Bundestag *Fraktion*'s paper 'Reflections on Europe' (the so-called Schäuble–Lamers paper).[13] The difficulty here, however, lies in deciding whether Klaus Kinkel was acting as spokesman for the policy of the Foreign Ministry or as Chairman of the FDP. It is clear that the policy ideas were generated in the Foreign Ministry, but the coalition agreement nevertheless allowed Kinkel to play the party card.

Of as much interest, but for a rather different reason, was the coalition agreement agreed by the SPD and the Greens in 1998, with Joschka Fischer at the helm of the Foreign Ministry. To some surprise, the broad thrust of foreign and European policy, as articulated by Fischer, was one marked by continuity.[14] Ignoring his party's former policy positions of withdrawal from NATO and deep suspicion of EU integration, Fischer sought with some success to project a basic sense of predictability in Germany's foreign policy role and commitments. 'The new federal government will', the SPD–Green coalition agreement promised, 'further develop the guidelines of previous German foreign policy.'[15] In the subsequent government declaration, it was underlined that 'we will meet our obligations in the framework of our alliances. We will remain reliable partners in Europe and the world.'[16] In the field of EU policy more specifically, the initial policy statements of the coalition extended at times beyond mere continuity into an almost ritualistic restatement of the existing priorities hitherto pursued by the Kohl governments:

> The integration of Germany in the European Union is of central importance for German politics. The new federal government will therefore push on the European integration process with new initiatives and use the German Presidency in the first six months of 1999 to bring new impulses to the deepening and widening of the European Union.[17]
>
> German–French friendship is the foundation of our European policy.[18]
>
> The historic opportunity of an enlargement of the European Union must be exploited with determination. The new federal government will actively support the European Union in this and will contribute to the economic and democratic stabilisation of the central and east European states via an effective accession strategy and solidaristic aid.[19]

This reaffirmation of old orthodoxies confirmed Fischer's success in manoeuvring the Greens (at elite level at least) into the heart of the Federal Republic's postwar consensus. In consequence, the only obvious example of party-political disagreement in recent years (notwithstanding the flirtations of the SPD with EMU scepticism as a means of recouping electoral ground – see Chapter 5) was in relation to Croatia, where the conversion of the SPD and the CDU/CSU at parliamentary level to the primacy of recognition left FDP Foreign Minister Genscher isolated in the Summer of 1991 and culminated in a pro-recognition policy so forceful as to box in Germany's partners and leave them with no alternative but to recognise Croatia. It is worth stressing at this point that the argument of this book has been focused on Germany's policy of pursuing milieu goals in a multilateral mode. Under party pressure on the Croatian issue, the Foreign Minister pursued a milieu goal through pressuring its partners in a much more unilateral mode. This unilateral action was, though, a clear exception to Germany's usual mode of operation in the EU and remains an isolated example of German assertiveness. Its significance lies less in unilateralism as such, and more in its illustration of the role that political parties can on occasion play in shaping the policy agenda and establishing a momentum for policy change which ministers may find difficult to resist. A rather more subtle form of agenda-shaping is conducted in the external arena.

External projection
Viewed from the outside and perhaps especially from the UK, political parties play a positive and important role in projecting Germany's milieu goals. There are a number of ways in which this is accomplished. First, German political parties are deeply embedded, and are indeed the major players, in their respective European-level party federations and this provides an alternative channel for influence. The obvious contrast here is with the rather isolated position of (pre-1997) UK governments which had to rely more or less exclusively on intergovernmental fora (although the post-1997 Labour government has placed itself in a position much more analogous to its German counterparts as a major player in the Socialist Group and in the Socialist International). The influence of transnational parties became apparent during the negotiations and ratification of the TEU. The explicitly political nature of the agenda for the pre-Maastricht IGCs meant that the actors in the IGCs were keen to seek alliances along ideological lines flanking their pursuit of national interests in the negotiation process itself.

Second, because the outcomes of IGCs have to be ratified in all the member states' legislatures and in a number of member states also by referenda procedure, the national political parties – especially those in opposition – were keen to secure input. Summits of federation party leaders held before each European Council thus became clearing houses during both the pre-Maastricht and pre-Amsterdam IGCs for the development of joint policies. The pre-summit meetings were often extremely influential. For example, during the EMU IGC in 1990, the setting of a fixed timetable for EMU was an important priority for Chancellor Kohl and the CDU/CSU. At the European People's Party (EPP) summit of national party leaders on 25 October 1990, the Christian Democrat leaders, including six heads of government, agreed unanimously to support the policy of the fixed timetable for EMU at the ensuing Rome Summit of 27 October 1990. Tellingly, the UK government had underestimated the importance of the EPP meeting, leaving Mrs Thatcher defeated and isolated at Rome. Similarly, the summit of Social Democratic party and government leaders in Malmo in June 1997 provided an opportunity while in opposition for the SPD to canvass support for its concern to have employment policy upgraded in the EU's list of priorities.

Third, party channels may be used as an alternative route for 'flying' bilateral European initiatives. A prominent example was the Blair–Schröder paper of June 1999 on Social Democratic modernisation. This presented a largely deregulationist modernisation agenda focused at the European level on countering the interventionist instincts of other left-led governments in the EU (notably in France).[20] The paper was effectively a joint enterprise of the respective heads of government, drafted by their chiefs of staff (Peter Mandelson/Lord Falconer and Bodo Hombach, respectively). It was, however, launched outside of formal government channels at Labour Party headquarters in London and formally presented first in Germany to a meeting of the SPD Executive; these party fora served to keep the Blair–Schröder paper at arm's length from 'official' status and thus to allow a serious attempt at European agenda-setting appear 'merely' as a party-political 'kite-flying' exercise.

Fourth, the existence of the (party-) political foundations is a massive repository of influence for German views on European integration. The major foundations have offices in most national capitals where they act as a filter between the state in question and their German parent. It could be argued that this filter function is most important during the EU accession process and if we look at Germany and the East-Central European countries, it is difficult to overestimate the role that the foundations play in introducing the governing elites of these countries to German policies and policy-makers. Even in an established state like the UK they can play a crucial role as for instance in the role that the Konrad Adenauer Foundation played in launching John Major's new 'heart of Europe' policy in 1991. The importance of the foundation connection was symbolised by the location of the speech in the Adenauer Foundation headquarters in Sankt Augustin. It would have been more usual for a ruling Prime Minister to have chosen an official or neutral setting. Prior to winning power in 1997, Tony Blair, Robin Cook (the then Labour shadow Foreign Minister) and Gordon Brown (then shadow Chancellor of the Exchequer) also made major speeches to the Friedrich Ebert Foundation as a means of floating European policy ideas which the Labour Party proposed to pursue in government.

Finally, the prestige of the Federal Republic and its key role in EU decisions also meant in the Kohl era that, although the CDU/CSU did not provide the foreign minister, key figures like the then parliamentary party leader Wolfgang Schäuble and foreign policy spokesman Karl Lamers could have a significant impact in framing the European debate in other countries. At the same time, the Federal Government was able formally to distance itself from ideas emerging from the CDU/CSU that provoked controversy in other parts of the EU. The classic case was the CDU/CSU's 'Schäuble–Lamers paper' of September 1994 in which the controversial idea of a 'core Europe' was introduced amid some acrimony onto the integration agenda. While the views in the paper were widely held to be those of Kohl, the use of the party channel shielded the Federal Government from much of the ill-feeling felt on the part of those member states Schäuble and Lamers left out of the 'hard core'. It has hitherto been a striking feature of the new government that no equivalents of Schäuble and Lamers are available to the SPD; indeed, looking beyond such *éminences grises* as Egon Bahr and Karsten Voigt (whose eminence has brought with it an independent-mindedness not necessarily welcome in a governing party), the relative paucity of younger foreign policy experts in the SPD capable of performing a semi-official kite-flying role is striking.[21]

The Länder, cooperative federalism and European policy

It was noted above that the relaunching of the European integration process in the mid-1980s provided the opportunity for Kohl's Federal Government to pursue the milieu goals of shaping European-level institutional and policy decisions in a way conducive to German interests. The relaunch also, however, provided the opportunity for the German Länder to seek solutions for the perennial problem of the 'blindness' of the integration process to their internal competences and status. They used this opportunity to press two agendas for improving their input into EU decision-making. The first – and the one to which the Länder initially gave greater priority[22] – was directed at establishing a Union-wide framework for regional-level input into EU decision-making. Their ultimate vision here was one of a three-level Union in which the 'third', regional level would emerge to play a direct role in European decision-making alongside the 'second' (member state) and 'first' (Union) levels. This might be described as an attempt to engage in a form of milieu shaping which would be conducive to specific Länder interests. A step in this direction was the Committee of the Regions established in the TEU largely as a result of Länder pressure. Subsequent experience with the Committee has, however, been rather disappointing for the Länder. The Committee was endowed with only weak, consultative powers, and even these have proved difficult to mobilise in a way satisfactory to the Länder given the differences of interest which inevitably exist in a body comprising, at one end of the scale, Länder Minister-Presidents equipped with a clear territorial mandate and a well-developed administrative support structure in EU affairs and, at the other, English local councillors which lack either.[23] As a result, the Länder have to a large extent scaled back their commitment to the Committee of the Regions and the wider 'third level' vision, seeking instead to press their European policy concerns in the sense of the second agenda developed in the 1980s.

Under this 'European domestic policy' approach, the Länder presented the demand that European policy-making should no longer be considered in constitutional terms as *foreign* policy, and therefore a monopoly preserve of the Federal Government. Given that over 50 per cent of laws applied in Germany are of European rather than domestic origin, and that many of these concern areas of Länder domestic competence, the Western Länder demanded that they should have rights of input into framing these laws analogous to the rights they have in domestic legislation. Otherwise, they argued, their status as constitutionally entrenched and empowered decision-making bodies was likely to be eroded.

This notion of 'European domestic policy', rather to their surprise, was broadly accepted in the TEU ratification debates and constitutionally established in amendments to the Basic Law (largely in the new Article 23). Alongside a general right of information and consultation on EU matters (except those falling under the second pillar of Common Foreign and Security Policy), these constitutional amendments gave the Länder, acting collectively through the Bundesrat, the right in domestic policy formulation to bind the Federal Government to their view on European policy matters which in domestic terms would fall under their legislative or administrative competence. It also gave the Bundesrat-nominated Länder representatives the right to speak for the Federal Republic in the Council of Ministers on those policy matters where the Länder domestically have exclusive legislative competence. The latter right created an internal procedure to make use of the new possibility provided in the amended Article 146 of the EC Treaty (amended with clear German support born of strong Länder pressure) for sub-national government ministers to sit on the Council of Ministers.[24]

As a result of these constitutional changes, competence in European integration policy has in essence been transformed from a monopoly external competence of the Federal Government to become a shared competence of federation and Länder, structured in a way broadly analogous to the internal competence-sharing typically described as co-operative federalism. This extension of cooperative federalism to European policy raises a number of wider questions about the strategies and effectiveness of German European diplomacy. Most fundamentally, have the Länder established with these new powers an unprecedented veto point on the integration strategies pursued by the Federal Government? Or, conversely, do the formal institutional constraints posed by the Länder powers act as facilitators for the wider strategic pursuit of German milieu goals? And at a tactical level, have the constraints inherent in enhanced Länder powers exacerbated the characteristic tactical weaknesses of German European policy engagement by impeding the presentation of clear German policy priorities in day-to-day EU decision-making?

The operation of Länder powers under Article 23
To address these questions requires a stocktaking of the Article 23 powers, in particular of the extent to which they have in practice constrained the wider thrust of Federal Government EU policy-making and/or compounded the problems of sectorisation noted earlier by adding new voices to the polyphony[25] already purporting to represent German interests in European decision-making.

There can be no doubt that, at a formal level, the Länder have won greater rights of input into European decision-making than any other sub-national governmental tier in the EU bar that of Belgium.[26] The extent to which those rights can be mobilised in practice is less clear. There are two main question marks. First, do the Länder have the administrative capacity to devote sufficient attention to the wide range of European legislation over which Article 23 powers give them rights of consultation and/or co-decision? Second, Article 23 sets out a collective decision-making process for the Länder. Their channel of input is the *collective* body of the Bundesrat. Can the Länder generate a sufficient unity of purpose to make full use of their collectively exercised powers?

The EU policy rights of the Länder immerse them in deliberations across a large and diverse number of policy fields.[27] And they are well supplied with information on EU policy developments at almost all the stages in policy-making in these fields,[28] the only significant exception being that the Länder have no direct access to top-level meetings of COREPER. The crucial issue is whether the scale of the information the Länder have to engage with across such a breadth of policy fields is too much for them to cope with in administrative terms, especially since the timescale for response to, and, by implication, influence on, EU matters is typically short (normally in a three-week cycle). It has certainly been suggested that 'the Länder have gained more extensive participatory rights than they can use effectively, given their limited administrative capacity for dealing with EU issues'.[29] There is certainly a kernel of truth in this suggestion, though it would be wise not to overgeneralise, since the Länder have done much over the last ten years purposefully to focus their internal administration and their collective decision-making structures on EU matters.

Internally, all Länder ministries now typically have officials dealing with European policy matters impinging on the departmental remit. Moreover, overarching responsibility for the development and management of European policy has been located in all the Länder in ministries (or sections of ministries) dealing with European affairs, to which Liaison Offices in Brussels have been attached. However, differences inevitably exist between the Länder in the effectiveness of these structures. European ministries have a remit which cuts across those of other ministries. Coordination of a general thrust in European policy can be difficult. Turf battles frequently ensue over European-related matters in a replica of the kind of policy sectorisation which has long been identified at the federal level. And – like the Foreign Office at the federal level – the European ministries in the Länder have only a limited sense of authority to bring to bear in cross-sectoral coordination. European ministries – like the Foreign Office – are of relatively low status, certainly ranking some way below Finance, Economics and Home Affairs. This is illustrated in the frequency with which European ministries have been reorganised following changes of composition of Länder governments, shunted around as a supplementary portfolio to Justice, Federal Affairs or Economics, or sucked into the Minister-President's Chancellery.

In these circumstances, the effectiveness of European policy administration in any one Land can vary widely. Two variables have a particular impact on the effectiveness equation.[30] The first concerns resources. Those Länder which invest heavily in European policy administrative infrastructure are better in the position to secure effective cross-sectoral coordination and develop clear and purposeful priorities. The capacity to invest varies, though broadly in relation to the wider financial situation of the Land concerned. Bremen and Saarland have, as a result, a rather indistinct and unassertive European policy profile.[31] At the other end of the spectrum, Bavaria, Baden-Württemberg, North Rhine-Westphalia and, to an increasing extent, Hesse, have been able to mobilise their superior resource base to establish an extensive European policy operation capable of effective policy coordination and presentation.

A further factor is the personal authority, interests and commitment of the relevant minister (or Minister-President) in European policy matters. Some of the smaller and financially weaker Länder have been able to 'punch above their weight' in EU matters by virtue of a weighty and/or well-connected personality. Examples would be the role played by the ex-MEP Gerd Walther in Schleswig-Holstein and the unobtrusive, but highly effective networking activities of the former State Secretary for European Affairs in Saxony-Anhalt, Rembert Behrendt.[32] The classic example, though, is Bavaria, where European policy is a responsibility of the Minister-President Edmund Stoiber's Chancellery, and whose European policy operation is generally acknowledged as the most tightly organised and effective among the Länder. This reflects Stoiber's degree of commitment to European policy matters and has resulted in a Bavarian European policy profile with an often international resonance.

Such factors also impinge in part on the collective capacity to coordinate Länder views in European affairs. Coordination takes place on two levels. First, the Committee for EU Affairs of the Bundesrat deals essentially with technical policy details. Second, a broader framework for coordination of political priorities exists in the Conference of European Ministers established in 1992. Both bodies are confronted in different ways with problems of sectorisation similar to those experienced within individual Länder. The Bundesrat EU Committee is the last of the Bundesrat committees to meet as preparations are made for each Bundesrat plenary meeting and has to weave into its deliberations the recommendations received from the other committees, some of which may have met only on the preceding day. Difficulties of coordination inevitably result. Similarly, the Conference of European Ministers holds meetings in parallel with the other sectoral ministerial conferences. Conflicts occur, and in their resolution the European Ministers are hampered by the same status deficit which exists within the individual Länder. Cross-sectoral coordination is as a result frequently sub-optimal. This broad tendency to sectorisation is compounded in those cases – which are not infrequent – when those Länder which lack an effective and systematic coordination procedure in internal matters end up supporting a position in a sectoral ministerial conference which conflicts with the position they support in the European Ministers' Conference.

A more fundamental problem facing the European policy coordinating bodies is that of divergent interests. This is less of a problem in the case of the largely technical issues discussed in the Bundesrat Committee, but is important in the more far-reaching political issues, normally dealt with in the European Ministers' Conference, which concern the broader role of the Länder in the European integration process. Examples would include structural funding, subsidy controls/competition policy and – as discussed in more depth in subsequent chapters – the 1996–97 IGC and eastern enlargement. There are broadly two poles of interest. At one end of the scale there are the 'big three' of Bavaria, Baden-Württemberg and North Rhine-Westphalia. These are always keen to point out that they have bigger populations and economies than a number of fully fledged EU member states and seek to play a decision-making role commensurate with their size and economic weight. They have placed particular emphasis on *competence assertion*, the defence of the remaining and few exclusive competencies of the Länder from erosion by growing European-level competence. The market leader here has certainly been Bavaria under Edmund Stoiber, whose trenchant views on reconstructing the scope of the Union are the closest a mainstream politician in Germany has come in approaching a UK-style Euro-scepticism. His central and recurring theme is one of curbing Commission intervention and regulation. It might be summarised in the phrase (with apologies to Lady Thatcher): 'I want my competences back'.[33] An especially vivid example was the 120-page dossier of alleged Commission infringements on the principle of subsidiarity Stoiber presented to then Chancellor Kohl in September 1998.[34]

At the other end of the spectrum lie the East German Länder. They are not especially interested in competence assertion or – notwithstanding the 'VW crisis' between Saxony and the Commission – the restriction of European intervention and regulation, for the simple reason that they cannot afford it. Just as in domestic politics, their economic weakness conditions an approach which rates financial support higher than preventing the erosion of competences.[35] An additional element of differentiation which paradoxically ranges the eastern Länder alongside Bavaria is eastern enlargement. This issue raises policy questions for those Länder on or near the enlargement border with Poland and the Czech Republic – on free movement of labour, internal security, locational competition – which simply do not exist for Länder further west.[36]

*Of strategy and tactics: federal–Länder interaction
in European policy*

These comments on administrative capacity and differentiation of interests allow a number of conclusions to be drawn about the impact in practice of Article 23 and more broadly about the nature of federal–Länder interaction in European policy. It is worth recalling some of the concerns expressed on the federal side at the time when Article 23 was being drafted. These recalled the spectre of a *Nebenaußenpolitik*, an 'auxiliary foreign policy' of the Länder, initially conjured up when they had first begun to demand access to European decision-making in the 1980s, which would restrict the Federal Government's freedom of manoeuvre in EC negotiations.[37]

Such fears were at the very least overstated. There have been no great trials of strength pitting Bundesrat against Federal Government in the exercise of Article 23 powers either in the Bundesrat coordination process internally or in the direct representation of Bundesrat nominees as part of the German delegation to the Council of Ministers. However, it is certainly the case that the problems of Länder coordination arising from sectorisation and differential administrative capacities can slow down the Federal Republic's speed of response in Brussels. A separate 'teething' problem which produced similar results was the initial inexperience (now largely rectified) of the Länder in decision-making processes in the Council. This led on occasion to the need to return to the Bundesrat to legitimate an emergent consensus view in the Council which did not accord with the formal and ostensibly non-negotiable position hitherto adopted by the Bundesrat internally. Such consequences of enhanced Länder input into European-level decisions may reinforce impressions of tactical weakness arising from lack of coherence in German European policy-making. Whether it undermines the Federal Government's freedom of action is less clear. Slowness of response may well allow the Federal Government the opportunity to set the agenda in a way which narrows the parameters of Länder influence. More generally, the pattern of divergence of Länder interests can act to water down, at least in politically controversial policy areas such as media policy or the Structural Funds, the policy positions they are able, through the Bundesrat, to present in European decision-making.

Impressions of a lack of coherence in German positions arising from Länder input may also act as a useful instrument for the Federal Government. The internal mechanics of cooperative federal arrangements in European policy are not easily penetrable for Germany's EU partners. This opacity may allow the Federal Government to defend its adherence to a certain position by claiming – with a certain economy with the truth – that it could otherwise not be 'sold' internally. If Germany's partners are forced to ask, as a senior German diplomat in Brussels noted, 'When will you know about whether this issue is settled?', because of the Federal Government's need to consult and coordinate with the Länder, a certain freedom of action is arguably *created* for the Federal Government. Whether, given its own problems of sectorisation and coordination, it is in the position to exploit this is a moot point. However, there remains a sense in which the density and complexity of Article 23 procedures have the capacity not to constrain the Federal Government, but to *empower* it in the pursuit of its strategic concerns by giving it a usable pretext that it can, on occasion, do nothing but represent unmovable domestic constraints in European-level negotiations.

'Institutional export' – Germany and the Treaty on European Union

The question of domestic constraints on German diplomacy in the EU needs not only to be addressed in the context of particular institutional interactions, but also in a wider sense. In a number of ways, the debates surrounding the TEU in the early part of the 1990s created a number of channels which have facilitated the exercise of 'institutional export', or what was termed in Chapter 1 indirect institutional power. The TEU debates revealed two forms of institutional export: those which emerged directly, in the course of European-level negotiation, in concrete features of the treaty text; and those which emerged indirectly in the course of domestic negotiation and debate on adapting the internal constitutional order to the external challenges posed by the accelerated integration process.

'Direct' institutional export

'Direct' institutional export has received the most attention, and relates to the influence of the Länder and the Bundesbank on the TEU text. In the TEU negotiations which culminated at Maastricht, the Länder were able to exert unprecedented influence over the treaty-making process. This reflected the fact that the treaty outcome would require constitutional changes internally and that such changes require two-thirds majority support in the Bundesrat. Given the success of the Länder in maintaining a unity of purpose in the debate about the future shape of European integration in the years following the SEA,[38] they were able to hang an entirely credible veto threat over the TEU ratification process. Seen in the wider context of the TEU negotiations – that of assuaging concerns over the impact of German unification through the pursuit of deeper European integration – a Länder-inspired German veto of the treaty was not something the Federal Government was willing to contemplate. The Länder were as a result given direct participation in the German negotiating team at the pre-Maastricht IGCs, and three of their four[39] core demands for the IGC on Political Union – subsidiarity, access to the Council of Ministers and the establishment of the Committee of the Regions – were ultimately incorporated into the TEU.[40] Nevertheless, they did achieve an at least partial sensitisation of European decision-making processes to the concerns they had about the previous incapacity of European-level decision-making to offer formal channels of input for sub-national entities; they can now present their concerns in the Council and through the Committee of the Regions (however weak its powers and diluted its composition), and they widened at least the terms of the debate (if not the treaty text) on subsidiarity to address not just member state–EU relations, but also the role of the sub-national level. Moreover, as significant as the treaty amendments was the mere fact of participation; future IGCs would also see attempts by the Länder to shape the institutional framework of the EU in a way compatible with their concerns. This is a question dealt with in Chapter 4 in the context of the 1996–97 IGC.

Of rather greater significance in terms of direct institutional export was the impact of the Bundesbank on the pre-Maastricht IGC on EMU. The Bundesbank provided for some years the prime example of the exercise of 'unintentional' power by German institutions in European policy-making. Its success in the pursuit of anti-inflationary *Stabilitätspolitik* and the consequent emergence of the DM alongside the dollar and the yen as one of the leading reserve currencies established it as an internationally powerful monetary policy actor. This power was reflected in the EU in the DM's role as the 'anchor' of the ERM of the EMS and most famously in the 'export' of the Bundesbank's stringent monetary policies in a way which contributed centrally to the exchange rate instabilities which culminated in the ERM crises of 1992–93. It was also reflected in the central role the Bundesbank assumed in directing the debate on EMU in Europe which took off with the appointment of the Delors Committee on EMU in 1988, and which set out a route to EMU in the TEU.

The Bundesbank's concern throughout was to ensure that a sufficient anti-inflationary ethos, capable of sustaining a rigorous *Stabilitätspolitik*, could be instilled into a future European Central Bank (ECB). And it broadly succeeded at Maastricht, where most of the technical conditions it had set out for the road to EMU were accepted, most notably an iron-clad guarantee of the independence of any ECB (to be located, of course, in Frankfurt) and of its commitment to *Stabilitätspolitik*, and the imposition of tough convergence criteria as preconditions for EMU membership. Indeed, in some respects, these guarantees were even firmer than those which the Bundesbank enjoys in German law. This allowed Helmut Kohl rightly to boast of the *deutsche Handschrift* on this part of the Treaty,[41] and presented an example of German institutional export of far-reaching significance for the future development of the EU.

However, any international treaty is inevitably a package of compromises. Consequently, other passages on EMU either bore the *Handschrift* of other member states and/or failed to meet Bundesbank demands. The Bundesbank had two particular concerns: that the timetable for achieving EMU laid out at Maastricht was unrealistic, and would lead to pressure to keep to timetable by easing the convergence criteria, notwithstanding the consequences this might have for the credibility of European-level *Stabilitätspolitik*; and that real progress towards the economic convergence necessary for EMU can only be made if parallel progress is made towards a more comprehensive Political Union capable of effective coordination of wider economic, fiscal and social policies. After Maastricht, the Bundesbank therefore continued to press these concerns in the EMU debates, continuing its attempt – discussed more fully in Chapter 5 – to secure for EMU a German-style institutional framework capable of replicating the monetary policy rigour it pursues 'at home'.

'Indirect' institutional export

The commitment of the Länder and the Bundesbank to 'direct' institutional export is overt and therefore relatively predictable. The same cannot be said for the potential for 'indirect' institutional export, which emerged in the TEU ratification process in Germany on the initiative of the Länder and the FCC. These initiatives led, in a mutually reinforcing way, to the establishment of general guidelines for the development of European integration, rooted in German constitutional practice, which, from a German perspective, may not be breached.

In respect of the Länder, the potential for indirect institutional export does not relate directly to the new rules on co-decision-making with the Federal Government established after Maastricht as a result of the new Article 23 of the Basic Law, and discussed in the previous section. These rules, to the extent that they Europeanise, and confront Germany's EU partners with, internal practices of cooperative federalism, are of course a form of institutional export. They have certainly changed the configuration of German actors with which Germany's partners have to engage. Essentially, though, they represent a new form of domestic decision-making which does not formally impact on the EU's institutional fabric. The form of institutional export with which the present discussion is concerned is rather different, and arises from the phrasing of Article 23, Paragraph 1, whose constitutional entrenchment was a trade-off by the Federal Government for Länder ratification of the TEU.

Article 23/1 was designed in one sense to provide safeguards additional to the new rights of co-decision awarded elsewhere in Article 23 against the erosion of Länder competences through closer European integration. It not only establishes a Bundesrat power of veto over transfers of sovereignty to the EU, but does so in a way which stipulates that any transfers which amend or supplement the content of the Basic Law are also subject to the provisions of Article 79/3 of the Basic Law. Article 79/3 – known as the 'eternity clause' – explicitly prohibits any amendments to the Basic Law which would have the effect of altering the federal structure of the Federal Republic. It also prohibits more broadly – and this is the wider sense in which the new Article 23 is so significant – any amendments which would impinge on a number of inviolable constitutional principles which underpin the Basic Law: federalism (again), democracy, the 'social state', the rule of law and human rights.

These inviolable principles receive further complementary protection in a so-called 'structural security clause' (*Struktursicherungsklausel*) in Article 23/1. This qualifies the commitment of the Federal Republic to 'participate in the development of a European Union' to the extent that the Union is 'committed to democratic, rule-of-law, social and federal principles as well as the principle of subsidiarity, and ensures protection of basic human rights comparable in substance to that afforded by this Basic Law'. With the exception of subsidiarity – whose appearance here is highly questionable[42] – these are again the principles singled out by Article 79/3 of the Basic Law as unamendable.

Article 23/1 thus stipulates that neither the transfer of sovereign powers (through the invocation of Article 79/3) nor the broader 'development' of the Union (through the *Struktursicherungsklausel*) may come into conflict with the fundamental principles of the Basic Law. These stipulations are innovations of potentially great constitutional importance. They were added to Article 23/1 as a means of drawing certain lines over which, from the German perspective, EU powers and regulations may not pass. This *no passaran* condition goes far beyond the mere protection of federalism, to imply more broadly that German constitutional organs have a right and duty to monitor and shape the future development of European integration in a far wider sense.[43]

This conditionality enables us to bring the FCC into consideration. The role of the FCC in European policy matters is necessarily somewhat opaque. Since European law is held to have primacy over domestic law, the role of interpreting the various European treaties and the legal acts based upon them falls, by general consent, to the European Court of Justice (ECJ). In this respect, the ECJ performs a role at the European level broadly equivalent to that the FCC performs in respect of the Basic Law in Germany. The FCC has, however, reserved for itself the right to question the primacy of European law over German law – and thereby the authority of the ECJ – if it feels European law is incapable of upholding the fundamental, inviolable constitutional principles of the Basic Law. This jurisprudence was revealed in the so-called *Solange I* judgment of 1974 in which a technical regulation of the CAP was held to demonstrate a potential incapacity of the EC to guarantee one of the inviolable principles of the Basic Law, that of the protection of basic human rights. This presumed incapacity led the FCC to claim for itself a monitoring role regarding the decisions of the ECJ in the field of human rights.[44]

The FCC's monitoring role was not subsequently mobilised in practice. The *Solange* judgment could best be seen as a 'warning shot' designed to encourage the ECJ to tighten up European human rights protection. Indeed, the FCC later renounced its monitoring role in the *Solange II* judgment of 1987, when it adjudged that sufficient guarantees of human rights had by that time been introduced into EC law. However, the *Solange* issues resurfaced in the FCC's judgment of 12 October 1993 on the compatibility of the TEU with the Basic Law.

Some twenty constitutional complaints were received by the FCC over the TEU. Most of these were dismissed by the Court as legally inadmissible. The exception was a part of the complaint made by Manfred Brunner, a former Commission official who had embarked on something of a crusade against the Maastricht Treaty. The admissible part of his complaint concerned the inviolable democratic principle of the Basic Law, in particular as expressed in Article 38. Article 38 stipulates the popular election of the Bundestag and implies, in the view of both Brunner and the Court, that the Bundestag should retain 'substantial' decision-making powers, otherwise popular participation in the democratic election process would be meaningless.

Brunner argued that the Maastricht Treaty in a number of ways, both directly and potentially, rendered the Bundestag's decision-making powers insubstantial and thus infringed the fundamental constitutional principle of democracy in Germany. In the end, the Court ruled[45] relatively straightforwardly that the Bundestag does for the time being retain sufficiently substantial powers to uphold the democratic principle in Germany. It also, less straightforwardly, laid down some markers to ensure that the democratic principle is maintained in the future. Most controversially, it echoed some of the issues in the *Solange I* judgment by setting out clear limits over which European organs may not pass without infringing the German democratic principle.

The guideline of the judgment was that European institutions may not exceed the powers explicitly covered in the TEU on the basis that it is the task of national parliaments to define the scope and purpose of the integration process and not the European institutions. Any European legislation or action which did exceed the bounds set out by treaty would, seen in this light, be invalid in Germany. The Court accordingly asserted – in a renewed challenge to the role of the ECJ – that it 'will examine whether legal acts of European institutions and organs are within the limits of the competences conceded to them, or whether they exceed those limits'.[46] Moreover, in more specific reference to the possibility of an EU *Kompetenz-Kompetenz*[47] emerging from Article F section 3 of the TEU, it authorised German state organs to 'deny obedience to legal acts based on such an application ...' of that Article.[48] This again assumes for the Court a role – the examination of the legal validity of EU actions, and the establishment of a right to ignore, where appropriate, actions deemed to be invalid – normally performed by the ECJ. This was widely regarded as 'a warning signal to the European Union to be more careful and stay within the bounds set by the treaties',[49] and more specifically to the ECJ to tone down its characteristic 'pro-integration activism', which has supported in the past an extensive interpretation of European-level powers to the chagrin of some member states. If the experience of the *Solange* jurisprudence is anything to go by, then the FCC's warning may well be heeded.

The FCC's TEU judgment has two further implications of significance for this discussion. The first is contained in the judgment and refers to EMU. Here, alongside a requirement that a German decision on joining EMU be confirmed in the Bundestag and may not simply occur 'automatically', even if the timetable and criteria set out in the TEU are met, the Court bizarrely raised the in political reality barely conceivable possibility of Germany leaving the EU should the EMU not prove capable of maintaining (an undefined level of) currency stability. This seems little more than an invitation for German constitutional complaints about the performance of a future ECB. It was a rather odd hostage to leave to future fortunes,[50] but was subsequently reinforced by comments emerging from the Court on the potential unconstitutionality of establishing an EMU which failed precisely to meet the convergence criteria set out in the TEU.[51] The predictable outcome was the series of constitutional complaints launched in the context of the German decision to join EMU, taken by an overwhelming Bundestag majority on 2 April 1998. This is an issue addressed further in Chapter 5.

A second implication of the FCC's apparent willingness to defend fundamental German constitutional principles against the infringements of the EU arises from the *no passaran* condition in Article 23/1, as discussed above (see p. 43). This stipulates that neither transfers of sovereign powers nor the broader 'development' of the Union may come into conflict with the inviolable principles underlying the Basic Law, i.e. democracy, guaranteed human rights, the rule of law and the federal and 'social' principles. Given the FCC's defence of the democratic principle in the Maastricht case and of human rights in the *Solange* cases, these must all be seen as potential 'hooks' on which constitutional complaints to supposedly 'unconstitutional' law can in future be hung.

It is, of course, uncertain whether and in what circumstances complaints might be hung on such hooks, and unclear as to how the FCC would react. The ultimately limited outcomes of the 1996–97 IGC (see further in Chapter 4) certainly offered no real opportunities for the FCC's position to be tested.[52] However, with Article 23/1 and the FCC's TEU judgment, a powerful set of parameters has been established which has the potential to *require* the integration process to proceed along routes essentially compatible with the German domestic constitutional order. That requirement will remain an important background condition for the development of the EU in the coming years.

The above discussion has shown that the externalisation of the internal peculiarities of the German system of government has impacted at the European level in two ways. First, the tradition of policy sectorisation, the role of the Bundesbank in monetary policy and the emergence of the Länder as co-decision-makers in a wide range of policy fields have complicated the process of arriving at clear German positions for presentation in routine decision-making, exacerbating the characteristic weakness and, on occasion, incoherence, of German negotiating *tactics*. Yet, second, externalisation has also strengthened the German *strategic* hand by imposing – or appearing to impose – immovable internal decision-making constraints on Germany's partners and by 'exporting' German institutional peculiarities into 'Europe' in a way which 'pays back',

European policy-making   47

in the sense of systemic empowerment by the institutional structure of the EU and thereby facilitates the pursuit of strategic German milieu goals. However, such goals ultimately can only be realised in interaction with other member states. The next chapter therefore sets out a number of illustrative examples of German alliance-building capacities in the EU.

Notes

1 See W. Paterson, 'The Chancellor and Foreign Policy', in S. Padgett (ed.), *Adenauer to Kohl: The Development of the German Chancellorship* (London: Hurst, 1994).
2 This situation becomes more complex under circumstances of co-habitation in France, such as following the election of the Socialist government headed by Lionel Jospin in June 1997.
3 See V. Busse, 'Regierungsbildung aus organisatorischer Sicht. Tatsächliche und rechtliche Betrachtungen am Beispiel des Regierungswechsels 1998', *Die Öffentliche Verwaltung*, 52 (1999), 317.
4 Confidential interviews conducted by Charlie Jeffery in Bonn, June 1999.
5 Cf. *Frankfurter Allgemeine Zeitung*, 22 June 1999.
6 See R. Hrbek, 'Eine politische Bewertung der VW-Beihilfen-Kontroverse', *Wirtschaftsdienst*, 10 (1996).
7 Confidential interviews conducted by Simon Bulmer in December 1996 in Whitehall.
8 See A. Nicholls, 'Germany and the European Union: Has Unification Altered Germany's European Policy?', *International House of Japan Bulletin*, 14 (1994).
9 'They do not strike the right tone in Brussels': in the words of one respondent in interviews conducted by Charlie Jeffery with representatives of other ministries in Bonn, June 1999.
10 The Economics-Environment conflict over regulation is one with a growing history. Cf. L. Andreae and K. Kaiser, 'Die "Außenpolitik" der Fachministerien', in W. Eberwein and K. Kaiser (eds), *Deutschlands neue Außenpolitik. Band 4: Institutionen und Ressourcen* (Munich: Oldenbourg, 1998).
11 This is a pattern persistent over time, as revealed in a series of semi-structured interviews conducted by Simon Bulmer in Bonn during 1994 and a further series conducted five years later by Charlie Jeffery in June 1999.
12 Such a case-by-case approach would, in any case, be likely both to seriously impede Germany's long-term strategic milieu goal of deeper European integration, and also to carry the risk, given Germany's existing preponderance as a trading state, of causing sufficient resentment in other member states to threaten German market access.
13 CDU/CSU *Fraktion des Bundestages*, *Überlegungen zur Europäischen Politik*, Bonn, 1 September 1994.
14 Entirely justifying Gunther Hellmann's comment that 'the most outstanding

characteristic of German foreign policy after 1990 has been continuity in the rhetoric of continuity'. Quoted in G. Hellmann, 'Nationale Normalität als Zukunft? Zur Außenpolitik der Berliner Republik', *Blätter für deutsche und internationale Politik*, 24 (1999), 837.

15 *Aufbruch und Erneuerung – Deutschlands Weg ins 21. Jahrhundert. Koalitionsvereinbarung zwischen der Sozialdemokratischen Partei Deutschlands und Bündnis 90/Die Grünen*, Bonn 20 October 1998 (hereafter Koalitionsvereinbarung), 41.

16 'Weil wir Deutschlands Kraft vertrauen.' Regierungserklärung des Bundeskanzlers vor dem Deutschen Bundestag. 10 November 1998 (hereafter Regierungserklärung), *Bulletin. Presse- und Informationsamt der Bundesregierung*. Nr. 74, 11 November 1998, 912.

17 Koalitionsvereinbarung, 41.

18 Regierungserklärung, 914.

19 Koalitionsvereinbarung, 42.

20 In the German context it also had the (desired) function of opening up what became a sustained and often bitter debate in the SPD on the purpose of economic and social policy. See C. Jeffery and V. Handl, 'Blair, Schröder and the Third Way', in L. Funk (ed.), *The Economics and Politics of the Third Way* (Hamburg: LIT-Verlag, 1999a).

21 As confirmed in an interview by Charlie Jeffery with a senior official of the Bundestag in June 1999.

22 C. Jeffery, 'Farewell the Third Level? The German Länder and the European Policy Process', *Regional and Federal Studies*, 6 (1996).

23 Piquantly, given the Federal Government's tradition of distaste for a greater role for the Länder in EU matters, the 'dilution' of the Committee of the Regions by the inclusion of local government representatives is said to have been a last-minute change decided with the purposeful connivance of Chancellor Kohl. See U. Kalbfleisch-Kottsieper, 'Fortentwicklung des Föderalismus in Europa – vom Provinzialismus zur stabilen politischen Perspektive?', *Die Öffentliche Verwaltung*, 46 (1993), 547.

24 Article 146 of the EC Treaty was renumbered Article 203 by the Amsterdam Treaty.

25 Bulmer and Paterson, *The Federal Republic of Germany and the European Community*, 19.

26 See B. Kerremans and J. Beyers, 'The Belgian Subnational Entities in the European Union: "Second" or "Third Level" Players', *Regional and Federal Studies*, 6 (1996).

27 As an illustration, the agenda for the meeting of the Bundesrat Committee for EU Affairs on 10 October 1996 covered the following: a prospective EU Association Agreement with Israel; trade in bananas; various foodstuffs; disability policy; conditions of service for Commission officials; consumer goods; legislative transparency in the Internal Market; transeuropean networks in the field of energy; refuse disposal; revitalisation of railways; forestry protection;

organic agriculture; animal diseases; a proposed European Agency for Veterinary Monitoring; semolina; nomination of representatives to advisory committees of the EU; and a partnership treaty with the Russian Federation.
28 The Liaison Offices they maintain in Brussels secure access to the early stages of policy formulation in the Commission. Well over 300 Länder officials are delegated to Commission and Council working groups. More recently, Länder officials have been seconded to the Permanent Representation in Brussels and participate in Foreign Office meetings which prepare instructions for German input into COREPER (though these officials do not have formal rights to pass on information to their Länder). Article 23 requires that the Federal Government pass on all the outputs of the policy process to the Bundesrat. In a limited number of policy fields Bundesrat-nominated representatives lead the German delegation in the Council (see below). And the Länder Observer in Brussels provides more general reports on Council business, although the significance of this longer-standing institution has been downgraded in the light of the other, more recently established information channels noted above.
29 K. Goetz, 'Integration Policy in a Europeanised State: Germany and the Intergovernmental Conference', *Journal of European Public Policy*, 3 (1996), 32.
30 For a fuller discussion of variables of effectiveness, see C. Jeffery, 'Sub-National Mobilisation and European Integration. Does it Make a Difference?', *Journal of Common Market Studies*, 38 (2000).
31 Perhaps surprisingly, the same does not apply so clearly in the case of the similarly impoverished East German Länder. In the process of administrative reconstruction after 1990, they placed heavy emphasis on developing solid European policy structures in the instrumental recognition that investment in 'Europe' would be paid back in the form of extensive structural funding.
32 Cf. C. Jeffery, 'Les Länder allemands et l'Europe: intérêts, stratégies et influence dans les politiques communautaires', in E. Negrier and B. Jouve (eds), *Que gouvernent les regions d'Europe* (Paris: L'Harmattan, 1998).
33 For example: 'Ich möchte ein höheres Maß an eigener Kompetenz haben für den Freistaat Bayern'. Quoted in *Süddeutsche Zeitung*, 8 May 1996, 28.
34 As reported in the Bavarian government publication *Europa aktuell*, September 1998.
35 One is tempted to recall here Brigid Laffan's memorable observation of Irish attitudes to the EU: 'While you're there in Brussels, get us a grant'. B. Laffan, '"While you're there in Brussels, get us a grant." The Management of the Structural Funds in Ireland', *Irish Political Studies*, 4 (1989).
36 Cf. C. Jeffery, 'The German Länder and the "Normalisation" of the EU Enlargement Debate', *Zentrum für Europäische Integrationsforschung, Bonn, Discussion Papers* (2000).
37 See e.g. O. Hahn, 'EG-Engagement der Länder: Lobbyismus oder Nebenaußenpolitik?', in R. Hrbek and U. Thaysen (eds), *Die deutschen Länder und*

die Europäischen Gemeinschaften (Baden-Baden: Nomos, 1986) and *Gemeinsame Verfassungskommission*, 2. Sitzung, 13 February 1992, 29; 3. Sitzung, 12 March 1992, 4, 16, 18 for a restatement.
38 C. Jeffery, 'The Länder Strike Back: Structures and Procedures of European Integration Policy-Making in the German Federal System', *Leicester University Discussion Papers in Federal Studies*, No. FS94/4 (1994), 7–9.
39 The fourth demand – that of a right of appeal to the European Court of Justice over supposed infringements of Länder competences by European institutions – was not successful, although a commitment on the part of the Federal Government to represent such appeals to the ECJ was later secured in internal negotiations.
40 Though not necessarily in the precise form they had wanted. See Jeffery, 'The Länder Strike Back', 10–12.
41 J. Sperling, 'German Foreign Policy after Unification: The End of Cheque Book Diplomacy', *West European Politics*, 17 (1994), 82–3; D. Marsh, *The Bundesbank: The Bank that Rules Europe* (London: Mandarin, 1993), 240.
42 The incorporation of the principle of subsidiarity into the *Struktursicherungsklausel* is incongruous. Its appearance alongside the inviolable principles of the German constitutional order suggests that it too holds similar rank. It does not. It is not even mentioned elsewhere in the Basic Law. This is not surprising since the term was not current when the Basic Law was framed. Moreover, the principle of subsidiarity – if it is to be understood, as the Länder have suggested, as a presumption for lower-level competence except when 'necessity' dictates higher-level intervention – is not reflected to any great extent in day-to-day politics in the German federal system. The German federal system is one predominantly geared to producing uniform national regulative standards, and the role of the Länder is primarily to co-determine those standards in cooperation with federal institutions rather than to exercise competences autonomously. See C. Jeffery, 'Plus ça Change ... The Non-Reform of the German Federal System after Unification', *Leicester University Discussion Papers in Federal Studies*, No. FS93/2 (1993).
43 G-B. Oschatz and H. Risse, 'Die Bundesregierung an der Kette der Länder? Zur europapolitischen Mitwirkung des Bundesrates', *Die Öffentliche Verwaltung*, 48 (1995), 438.
44 On the *Solange* judgments, see D. Wincott, 'Human Rights, Democracy and the Role of the Court of Justice in European Integration', *Democratisation*, 1 (1994), 255–65.
45 *Entscheidungen des Bundesverfassungsgerichts, 89. Band* (Tübingen, Mohr, 1994), Nr. 17, Urteil vom 12. Oktober 1993 (2 BvR 2134, 2159/92). Maastricht-Vertrag. A fuller analysis of the Court's ruling than can be given here can be found in G. Ress, 'The Constitution and the Maastricht Treaty: Between Cooperation and Conflict', *German Politics*, 3 (1994).
46 Quoted in Ress, 'The Constitution and the Maastricht Treaty', 62.
47 Only loosely translatable as a 'competence to establish (the scope of) compe-

tences', and more specifically in this context the capacity to impute from the EU's goals a legal competence to act not enshrined in the Treaty.
48 G. Ress, 'The Constitution and the Maastricht Treaty', 64.
49 Ibid., 67.
50 See *Süddeutsche Zeitung*, 9 October 1993, 2.
51 See the comments of Paul Kirchhof, FCC Justice, as reported in the *Wall Street Journal Europe*, 30 October 1996. This question is taken up further in Ch. 5.
52 Though it still did not prevent constitutional challenge. Cf. U. Karpenstein, 'Der Vertrag von Amsterdam im Lichte der Maastricht-Entscheidung des BVerfG', *Deutsches Verwaltungsblatt*, 17 (1998).

3
Relations with partners

Questions concerning Germany's relations with its partners, especially with those whose territory borders on Germany, have been central to German European policy since the establishment of the Federal Republic in 1949. The troubled history of the period between 1870 and 1945 and Germany's postwar status as an occupied, semi-sovereign state demanded a reformulation of Germany's relations with its Western neighbours. The then fragile and constrained Federal Republic had an elemental interest in changing the milieu in which it was embedded and this change had to begin with its neighbours. Adenauer's choice, which has been followed by all succeeding governments, was to reject even the theoretical possibility of Germany acting as a 'balancer between east and west' and to place Germany in the vanguard of those West European states which supported the project of European integration. Crucial to the success of this policy was close cooperation with France, since it was France at that time which was the main barrier to Germany's return to the status of international actor. However, while the origins of the relationship can be partially explained on the prudential grounds of removing an obstacle to Germany's participation internationally, it always had a strong symbolic content as emblematic of a new type of relationship between European states. As European integration progressed, it acquired increasing importance both in providing strategic leadership for the Community and as the site for many of the tactical deals which European policy demands.

For much of the history of European integration, German European policy was remarkable less for the way it handled relations with its partners, save for the Franco–German relationship, than for its commitment to European institutions as the locus of policy-making. Germany's identity as a reflexive multilateralist was constructed through its European policy and 'in the eyes of German political elites, institutional memberships were not merely instruments of policy but also normative frameworks for policy-making'.[1]

This meant that to an unusual degree much of the onus in mediating the relationship with its neighbours rested in Bonn's view on the Community institutions, especially the Commission. While this was the overall stance, it was of course subject to fluctuation, depending on the strength of the European commitment of the Federal Chancellor and the leadership of the Commission. It reached a low point under Helmut Schmidt, but was again important in the Delors Presidency, where his support was to prove vital to the Kohl government on a number of occasions, most notably the negotiations concerning German unity.

The relationship with France established a settled German preference for strategic partnerships, based on a long-term commitment to a strategic project rather than growing out of agreement on a range of technical issues. A virtuous circle is thereby established: the partnership precedes agreement on issues; the existence of the partnership helps to bring about agreement on the issues; and agreement is sometimes reached for the sake of the partnership. In the old Europe of the six, the Franco–German relationship was 'the Privileged Partnership',[2] since the other member states generally tended to follow the Franco–German lead, though the Netherlands government was notably sceptical about the Fouchet Plan and De Gaulle's veto of British entry in 1963, and the 'empty chair policy' of 1965–66 also led to dissension in other member states, including Germany itself.

The position began to change from the mid-1980s onwards and the Federal Republic began to seek other strategic relationships. There are three obvious explanations for this change. First, the Community itself had become larger, more heterogeneous, more unpredictable and potentially less easy to manage on the basis of the Franco–German core. Second, the introduction of qualified majority voting (QMV) in the SEA (1986) opened up the possibility of a much greater dynamism in the EC and increased the chances of realising German aspirations to achieve the milieu goal of progressing towards much deeper European integration. A final factor was the strength of Helmut Kohl's commitment to European integration in the 1990s. While continuing to place the Franco–German relationship at the heart of his European diplomacy, Kohl clearly perceived that wider support would be necessary if integration were to proceed.

Germany's increasingly central role in the EU has also impacted on partnership strategies. For most of the history of European integration, Germany has forsworn a leadership role, preferring as a 'reflexive'[3] multilateralist to frame its preferences from within the context of multilateral institutions and to seek to shape the agenda through the Franco–German relationship. German unity appeared to many, especially to external observers, to open up the possibility of a much enlarged role for Germany, with some like William Wallace even talking of Germany as a 'natural hegemon'.[4] The principal reactions of the German government were to respond to these fears by advancing proposals to anchor Germany in a more deeply integrated Europe and to devote even more attention to its partners. This could be seen very clearly in the efforts in the mid-1990s to assuage French concerns about the pace and motives of German support of EU enlargement (see Chapter 6). It could also be seen in a growing sensitivity to the concerns of smaller member states, especially since the first Danish Referendum on the TEU in June 1992. From that point on 'small state diplomacy' was intensified in a widening rota of visits and bilaterals, while Germany also became especially careful not to appear to preempt the role of the Presidency of the EU Council by too much reliance on Franco–German *démarches* when the Presidency is held by one of the smaller states. A similar pattern of preference for long-term strategic relationships has appeared in a weakened form in relation to the applicant countries, with the German–Polish relationship often privileged in policy declarations.

The impact of the change of government in 1998 on Germany's partnership strategies has not yet crystallised into a clear pattern. Early indications suggest though that Gerhard Schröder has a more open alliance strategy which may weaken the exclusivity of the Franco–German core relationship and generate alternative and, possibly, competing partnership opportunities. A much closer attention to the UK–German relationship – facilitated, of course, by the more positive attitude of the Blair government to the EU – is a notable example of the potential for diversification under Schröder.

In the following, we present a more detailed analysis of Germany's relations with an illustrative selection of EU partners:

- first, the Franco–German relationship, Germany's defining strategic partnership in the EU,
- second the German–Dutch relationship, which has moved from a conventional to a deeper relationship, and
- third, the German–British relationship, which has more recently

moved onto a stronger footing, having hitherto represented a clear case of failure to establish a strategic partnership

The Franco–German relationship

The Franco–German relationship has been at the core of German European policy since its inception. While it largely rests on converging interests, the relationship has often seemed to become a value in itself, at least for the German participants, and as being special in the sense of transcending interests.

The Franco–German relationship not only provided the key to lifting discriminatory provisions on Germany's coal, coke and steel industries through the Schuman Plan (many of these provisions had been there to assuage French fears), but is at the centre of the view of the EU as a *Werte- und Friedensgemeinschaft* which continues to be a powerful force in German European policy, with the Franco–German relationship as its most potent symbol.[5] Joseph Weiler has written of the founding and legitimating concepts of postwar European integration and the Franco–German relationship has been seen as central to two of the central concepts, peace and prosperity.[6]

The Franco–German relationship was central to Adenauer's Rhineland conception of Europe, convinced as he was that France was the key to deeper European integration and German rehabilitation. Given the politics of the Fourth Republic, this relationship was not free of strain and Adenauer was deeply disappointed over the failure of the European Defence Community (EDC) to survive in the *Assemblée Nationale* after he had invested so much political capital in the project inside Germany. In 1953 when it was already under pressure, Adenauer said to his CDU colleagues, 'I would very much welcome a certain British influence in the future EDC so that we are not left alone with the more or less hysterical French'.[7] Adenauer's guiding and incontrovertible instinct was, however, that France was central to the European project and German negotiators, conscious of the failure of the EDC and the weakness of the French government(s), were prepared to make concessions in the European Economic Community (EEC) negotiations. It is sometimes argued that the CAP was among these concessions, but here it is more accurate to talk of a Franco–German convergence with German farmers, if anything, having at the time a stronger interest in high-cost agriculture.

From the late 1960s, the Franco–German relationship, constrained as it was by the Luxembourg Compromise of 1966, lost much of the motor function it had acquired under Adenauer, but it became increasingly crucial again during the Schmidt Chancellorship. Helmut Schmidt was even more strongly convinced than other German leaders that unilateral action by the Federal Government would necessarily arouse opposition among Germany's partners. He therefore followed a policy of bilateral *démarches* almost exclusively with France since, once Chancellor, he quickly came to abandon his earlier inclination to the UK. The early years of Schmidt's relationship with the French President Giscard d'Estaing saw a substantial thickening of the institutional underpinnings of the relationship, together with the creation of a system of governance at the European level in the European Council which empowered these procedural reforms. In the second half of the 1970s, the relationship spawned a series of initiatives, the most important of which was the EMS.

The downside of reliance on the Franco–German relationship was evident in the initial years of the Mitterrand–Kohl relationship, where the French government displayed little interest in European integration and German European policy was to some extent becalmed. The more pro-European policy of the Mitterrand government from 1984 onwards, the introduction of QMV after the passing of the SEA in 1986, and a facilitative President of the EC Commission in Jacques Delors restored a central role to the Franco–German motor. By the late 1980s, therefore, the Franco–German relationship had reached its present institutional form and exerted three mutually reinforcing pressures on German European policy. First, it institutionalised a Franco–German coordination reflex. This has ensured that both parties have normally been able to bring sufficient modifications to each other's European policies to avoid the open divergences of the mid-1960s. A second effect has been that German initiatives in the EC/EU have been presented overwhelmingly in Franco–German clothing. For historical reasons, successive German governments have avoided unilateral moves in European policy and the Franco–German relationship not only reflected this, but also provided a basis whereby the governments of the two largest EC economies could mobilise the EC policy process. As Helen Wallace put it, 'if a Franco–German deal could be stitched together even on issues difficult for one or both, the other participants in the negotiations would generally fall into line'.[8]

A third effect of the Franco–German relationship is to give some reinforcement to the sectorisation of Germany's European policy. The extensive bilateral discussions held at various levels between the two governments are essentially conducted on a specialist basis. There is no agency in Bonn with the task of checking whether views expressed by one federal minister to his French counterpart are compatible with those expressed by another German minister to *his* opposite number. The greater degree of centralisation in the French government ensures, by contrast, greater compatibility in the French case. Thus, to take the agricultural policy area, it would be possible for the German and French Agriculture Ministers to come to a close 'pre-understanding' on the CAP – but without necessarily ensuring that this agreement was adequately compatible with the overall objectives of German European policy. This pre-understanding would then have a privileged status because of its Franco–German character.

The Franco–German relationship has functioned very effectively as a strategic spine and provides a major explanation of the success of German European policy at a strategic level. It has formed the bedrock for progress towards deeper European integration and it was noticeable in the 1980s that the balance of adjustment in the relationship was borne increasingly by France whether the issue was Iberian enlargement, agricultural reform, the Uruguay Round negotiations or most fundamentally the French adoption of German monetary policy. Its record at a tactical level has been much more mixed, given the way it has fed, as noted above, into a pre-existing sectorisation in the German policy process, and its capacity to complicate relations with Germany's other partners, especially the UK.

The closeness of the Franco–German relationship is central to an understanding of German European policy after 1989. British and American fears about the potential threat posed by a united Germany were addressed by the inclusion of the whole of Germany within NATO. This policy could not be expected to assuage French fears either of a German *Alleingang* vis-à-vis the East or a German hegemon role within the EC. The response of the Kohl government – which reflected also its own preferences – was to anchor Germany more deeply in a more integrated Europe through treaty amendments following IGCs on EMU and Political Union. The question of EMU was regarded as being particularly important in ameliorating French fears and the whole development of the EMU project has been 'nested' in the Franco–German relationship. The outcome of the Maastricht negotiations was a mixed balance sheet for the Franco–German relationship. On EMU, where much of the preliminary work had been done by the Delors Committee and where both states were 'singing from the same hymn sheet', progress was very impressive, but on Political Union, where the French government had reservations, progress was far slower.

The advent of President Chirac put some strains on the relationship and his heroic style of leadership put rather less emphasis on the coordination reflex. This has administered a number of shocks to the relationship, largely in the security area where President Chirac has shown a fondness for 'lonely decisions' in the form of moves towards security cooperation with the UK (culminating in the Franco–British St Malo Declaration on European defence identity in December 1998).[9]

At the Amsterdam IGC there appeared, in contrast to Maastricht, to be fewer areas of Franco–German convergence (see Chapter 4). In particular, there was no equivalent to EMU as *le grand projet*, which had been largely worked on and agreed by the French and German governments pre-Maastricht. Nevertheless, as was noted in Chapter 1, the Franco–German *démarche* remained the preferred route and this, of course, has traditionally served to privilege issues on which agreement between the two governments exists and to bracket out issues on which they disagree. The defining issue, however, remained EMU, where the Federal Government had staked a great deal on the resolution of the French government to push the project through. That issue was complicated by President Chirac's decision to go for an early election in 1997 and – contrary to Chirac's calculations – the Socialist government headed by Prime Minister Lionel Jospin which was returned. 'Cohabitation' in French government inevitably complicates Franco–German relations, and the composition of the new government had particular implications in this respect for EMU, with Jospin's government seeking to impose the trade-off of action on the employment question within the framework of continuing, parallel discussions on EMU. Given the budgetary pressures on the German government, this was not a welcome initiative, and is discussed further in Chapter 4.

The prospect of a Schröder-led government aroused considerable anxiety in Paris, though French fears were quickly assuaged after September 1998. The new Finance Minister and then SPD party chairman, Oskar Lafontaine had a great deal of latitude given the strength of the SPD and the weakness of its coalition partner and his priority was to increase cooperation with Dominique Strauss-Kahn, the French Finance Minister, in pursuit of his neo-Keynesian policies. At the same time, Joschka Fischer, the new Foreign Minister, restated classic goals of German European policy in a way at times reminiscent of Kohl in his visionary mode. He expressed particular commitments to EMU, further constitutionalisation of the EU, and to the Franco–German relationship. The strength of the latter commitment was confirmed by an unchanged frequency of institutional contacts and the appointment of Brigitte Sauzay, President Mitterrand's German-born interpreter, as adviser on European policy. Strains were however imported via Chancellor Schröder's frequent statements about reducing Germany's net budgetary contribution – with inevitable implications for France and the budget-consuming CAP from which it benefited. While these strains did not imply any change in the priority that the German government accorded to the Franco–German relationship, they did become increasingly hard to accommodate, in particular as they became concretised in the difficult negotiations surrounding the Agenda 2000 package of budget and policy reform. A significant reduction in Germany's net contribution as part of this package realistically necessitated a major reform of the CAP, which the new government – lacking the dependence of its predecessor on the agricultural vote – was keen to pursue, in particular via a new national co-financing arrangement for farming support. Co-financing was, however, anathema to the French government and was effectively vetoed by Chirac amid considerable Franco–German tension (see Chapter 6).

The Franco–German relationship remains, though, Germany's preferred strategic partnership and is still crucial on issues like EMU. It is also normatively and institutionally so securely anchored that it is virtually impregnable against a direct assault. The result is an underlying continuity in the Schröder government's stance on the Franco–German relationship. Any direct assault would unleash deep resentment in France, where the symbolic importance attached to it is an important aid to France accepting change in the balance of adjustment between the two states which was noted above. If it is impregnable to a direct assault, though, there are a number of senses in which it is becoming much more exposed. Eastern enlargement of the EU is certainly one, opening up opportunities for Germany unavailable to France and shifting the centre of gravity of the Union north-eastwards (see Chapter 6). Perhaps even more importantly, globalisation has brought about important changes in Germany's political economy. Massive mergers involving defining German firms like Daimler-Benz and Deutsche Bank have taken place. These mergers have followed the logic of globalisation rather than EMU and have been across the Atlantic rather than across the Rhine. German business, which has been among the most pro-European of a hitherto Europeanised elite, now has wider interests and in trade issues is likely to throw its weight much more decisively than before in an Anglo-Saxon rather than continental/protectionist direction. Initiatives like the joint paper published by Prime Minister

Blair and Chancellor Schröder (see p. 69) confirm this shifting perspective.

In summary, the Franco–German relationship has been crucial to Germany in its integrationist mode and central to shaping the regional milieu through projects like EMU. If EMU operates with an expansive logic, it will remain so. Beyond EMU, however, it is becoming much more difficult to discern projects of which the Franco–German relationship will necessarily remain at the heart.

German–Dutch relations

The German–Dutch relationship, which has acquired increasing importance in German European policy, illustrates the importance that the Federal Government attaches to strategic partnerships and the reliance it places on governing elites in partner states in order to realise its policy goals. This is all the more the case given that German–Dutch relations in the postwar era were perhaps more deeply affected by the trauma of German invasion and occupation than in any other of the original member states. This wartime experience discredited neutrality as a foreign policy stance in the Netherlands, and Dutch governments, like their German counterparts, became reflexive multilateralists in NATO and the EEC. The Dutch economy also became ever more closely interlocked with that of Germany. Despite this wide-ranging elite convergence, differences remained. The Dutch were much more consistently supportive of a liberal external trading policy than were successive German governments. The Dutch commitment to European institutions rendered them also at times resentful of the Franco–German partnership. Their commitment to a liberal trading policy and the importance of transatlantic links also rendered them particularly sympathetic to British entry. And although the German–Dutch relationship functioned well, despite occasional divergences, at the elite level, Dutch popular opinion remained notable for its generally suspicious set of attitudes towards Germany and this suspicion did not decrease in the years of joint participation in European institutions.

This pattern of relationships where elite relations were characterised by 'reason' (*Vernunft*) and popular attitudes by suspicion might well have persisted indefinitely had it not been for the shock of unity. German unity intensified both Dutch popular suspicions and set in train a series of disagreements at the governmental elite level, which were to plague relations for the next three to four years. Relations between Prime Minister Ruud

Lubbers and Chancellor Kohl, already strained by conflicts with Kohl in the context of the meetings of the European Christian Democratic leaders, where Kohl had objected on occasion to Lubbers' style of chairing meetings, were exacerbated further by Lubbers' lack of enthusiasm for German unity and his readiness to extend a sympathetic ear to Mrs Thatcher's even more decided hostility. While Lubbers, like other leaders including Andreotti, Mitterrand and even Mrs Thatcher, eventually rallied behind the German unity process, his stance fed into an increasingly difficult relationship between himself and Chancellor Kohl. Lubbers occasioned particular annoyance by his criticism of what he saw as temporising on the Oder–Neisse frontier where he called for 'respect for territorial boundaries as they now are', a view which prompted Chancellor Kohl to retort 'that he Lubbers had not learnt the lessons of history'.[10]

Relations between the Foreign Ministers Hans Dietrich Genscher and Hans van den Broek were also frequently reported as being very cool.[11] They worsened in the run up to the Maastricht Treaty negotiations. The Luxembourg government, which occupied the Presidency in the first half of 1991, had produced a cautious 'non-paper' as a draft of the TEU. Piet Dankert, the Netherlands Minister for European Affairs, believing he had been encouraged by the German government to produce a more ambitious draft, unveiled a much more federalist version in early September 1991. At the Council of Foreign Ministers meeting called to discuss this plan on 30 September 1991, to the intense chagrin of the Dutch government, their only support came from the Belgian government and the Maastricht Treaty as finally negotiated was much closer to the Luxembourg draft.

Whether or not the German government had in fact given Piet Dankert the encouragement he claims, it would have been discouraged from supporting an isolated Dutch position after its experience at the European Council of Finance Ministers (ECOFIN) meeting on 9 September 1991 where the German government was the only one to support an explicit two-speed model for EMU put forward by the Dutch Finance Minister Wim Kok. The meeting was reportedly very acrimonious and Kok eventually disowned responsibility for the draft.

In a hard-hitting speech at the *Evangelische Akademie* at Tutzing on 15 January 1992, Piet Dankert reflected deep Dutch disappointment with recent German policy: 'I would not be faithful to Dutch policy, if I did not tell you how much we regretted the absence of German support for the earlier Dutch treaty draft.'[12] On the recognition of Croatia and Slovenia Dankert argued further:

On the German side this was argued for very strongly with the accent being laid on strong language rather than convincing arguments. Often it appeared *as if it were more about the recognition of Germany than Croatia.* This was a very unfortunate beginning for a Common Foreign and Security Policy for which the Maastricht Summit had just opened the way. It would have reflected well on the German government if it had defended the Dutch Presidency against unjustified and vile attacks from sections of the German media. European solidarity can in the last analysis not come from one side alone.[13]

There were also significant German–Dutch differences over the future position of the Western European Union (WEU) in the Maastricht negotiations, where Dutch negotiators were notably sympathetic to Anglo-American anxieties about a weakening of NATO should WEU be moved too far in the direction of integration into the EU. Relations deteriorated further over the question of the siting of the ECB where Prime Minister Lubbers insisted in 1993 on the candidature of Amsterdam long after it was clear that the only possible choice was Frankfurt. And a final twist in the downward spiral of relations was given by Chancellor Kohl's opposition to Ruud Lubbers' bid to succeed Jacques Delors as President of the European Commission at the Corfu Summit 1994. Lubbers was widely regarded as heir-apparent to Delors and had announced in 1993 that he would not seek a fourth term as Prime Minister (i.e. beyond the 1994 election) with the unspoken sub-text that this would leave him free to become EU Commission President. The manner in which the decision to reject Lubbers in favour of the Belgian Prime Minister Jean-Luc Dehaene[14] appeared to have been taken – by a Franco–German *directoire* – caused serious offence in the Netherlands.

These divergences at governing elite level were flanked by very worrying trends in Dutch public opinion. In a study undertaken by the Clingendael Institute between November 1992 and January 1993 on the views of Dutch youth, it was striking that under the influence of both family memories of the occupation and a heavily publicised series of attacks on foreigners in Germany, most notably in the towns of Mölln and Hoyerswerda, they had a very negative view of Germany, and 60 per cent thought of Germans as arrogant, while 71 per cent regarded them as too dominant.[15]

This cycle of deteriorating relations between the two states has been turned around by determined action by both governing elites. The Lubbers affair acted as a catalyst for both partners. On the Dutch side the Clingendael survey also had an impact. The conclusions that the Dutch elite drew from the Lubbers affair after they had got over their initial wounded pride were:

- even if they did not like the idea of a *directoire*, the Netherlands was not going to make much impact if they found themselves permanently in opposition to Franco–German positions;
- the British government was a fairly unreliable partner and in any case 'the Netherlands should orient itself towards the centre of Europe, not its periphery'.[16]

Van den Broek's successor as Dutch Foreign Minister, Pieter Kooijmans, was reputed in this context as saying: 'The Germans can live without the Dutch, but the Dutch cannot live without the Germans.'[17]

On the German side there was some alarm at the fall out from the Lubbers affair and at the results of the Clingendael investigation and the Federal Government set out together with the new Kok government to reinvent the German–Dutch relationship. Perhaps the most important initiative was to create the first German–Dutch Corps, which includes the entire Dutch army. Although initially led by a Dutch commander when it was inaugurated in Münster in 1995, his successor will be German. It was decided also to launch a German–Dutch elite-level conference to encourage elite bonding. This met first in Delft on 21–22 March 1996. There was also an intensification of visits beginning with Chancellor Kohl's visit to Rotterdam in May 1995 and President Herzog's two-day visit in October 1995. The reciprocal visits culminated with the award of the *Karlspreis* to Queen Beatrix on 16 May 1996. Chancellor Kohl had closer relations with Kok and their respective Foreign Ministers also had a cordial relationship. Overall the response of the Dutch government was not only to align its policy much more closely with the German government, but also greatly strengthen the institutional underpinnings of the relationship.

The reinvention of the Dutch–German relationship must be accounted a success. In the run up to the 1996–97 IGC, the contrast with Maastricht was striking and the convergence between Dutch and German positions very noticeable. Few public fears are now expressed in Holland about German domination in Europe; indeed, it has now become more common for Dutch official spokesmen to ask for Germany to take on a greater leadership role.[18] Moreover, the Netherlands were conspicuous as a supporter of Germany in the proposals for a Stability Pact in the parallel EMU negotiations. Dutch support for the German position on EMU was reflected in the Federal Government throwing its weight behind the Dutch candidate for the first head of the ECB, Wim

Duisenberg. This success was only possible, however, because of the actions of the Dutch elite who, when confronted with a public opinion hostile to Germany, instead of trying to make electoral capital out of it, laboured together with the German government to forge a strategic partnership of policy alignment and a deeper institutional relationship.

The German–British relationship

The German–British relationship before the election of the Labour government under Tony Blair in 1997 is the most striking example of a failed attempt to form a strategic partnership. To understand the reasons why that attempt was always likely to fail requires some analysis of the evolution of the relationship. While a strategic partnership based on a shared perception of interests and common assumptions about the NATO structure proved relatively easy to achieve, European integration has normally been a divisive issue between the two states.[19] Although the German government supported the first British application for EEC membership, there was disappointment and resentment on the British side that ultimately the imperatives of the Franco–German relationship were seen as more pressing. British attempts – as in the second application – to utilise Britain's strategic NATO partnership and the British Army on the Rhine to press the entry application were a failure and caused considerable resentment on the German side.

In the two decades following British entry to the EEC, British–German differences on European integration rarely, except for some acrimony over the question of the UK budget rebate, led to crisis in the relationship, since the Luxembourg Compromise and the Gaullist legacy in France prevented the EC developing at a speed and in ways which British governments would have found threatening. The passing of the SEA, the subsequent extension of QMV, and Franco–German agreement on much deeper integration, together with the presence of Jacques Delors as Commission President, put the Thatcher government under increasing pressure in the late 1980s. The result was to expose deepening UK–German divergences, with Mrs Thatcher spending much more time in attempting to cultivate President Mitterrand than Chancellor Kohl.

The defining event in the relationship, however, was German unity. The then Prime Minister, Margaret Thatcher, viewed the world through a realist prism and the increase in power of one state necessarily involved the diminution in power of another. 'Germany got bigger and we didn't', as she was wont to say.[20] On the issue of German unity, Thatcher, by that time a dominating force in her government, took a more hostile line than the UK Foreign Office, and it was her view that prevailed. There is also a strong British tradition of balance of power thinking and the emergence of a potentially dominant Germany on the European mainland excited great anxieties. Thatcher initially entertained hopes, not entirely without foundation, that she would be able to detach President Mitterrand, but this fairly soon proved to be a cul de sac and the strength of American backing for German unification rendered unity inevitable. For his part, Chancellor Kohl was disappointed in what he saw as a British failure to live up to their treaty promises of support for German unity. He shared British fears of a potentially dominant Germany and sought the remedy in much deeper European integration and in German *Einbindung* into integrated structures. While this policy prevailed and preparations were set in train for the IGCs on Political Union and EMU, the prescription found little favour with Mrs Thatcher:

> Some people say you only need to anchor Germany in Europe if you want to avoid the character traits of her political overweight (*Übergewicht*) to reassert themselves. But no – rather than Germany within Europe, it is Europe we have anchored to a newly dominant Germany. Therefore I call this a German Europe.[21]

Prime Minister Thatcher's reservations were widely known at the time and the conclusions of a seminar convened by her at Chequers on 24 March 1990, the weekend before she was to meet Chancellor Kohl at the Königswinter Conference in Cambridge, and then in London for a bilateral, were widely leaked. In the memorandum of the meeting, the German character was identified with 'angst, aggressiveness, assertiveness, bullying, egotism, inferiority complex, and sentimentality.'[22] Relations were further damaged by an interview given by Nicholas Ridley, a member of the Cabinet, and close ally of Mrs Thatcher, where he referred to EMU as 'a German racket designed to take over the whole of Europe'.[23]

Defeated on German unity and alarmed by the pace of European integration and unpopular at home, Mrs Thatcher became an embattled Prime Minister. Her increasingly intemperate and outspoken opposition to developments in European integration generated increasing anxiety that her policies were deeply damaging to UK interests, and that in pursuing sovereignty and identity so fervently, she was in danger of excluding Britain from any real influence in the Community and risking the real and tangible interests of the City of London and other economic interests. These anxieties, compounded by a sense that she and her 'flagship' domestic policy – the flat-rate 'poll tax' for financing local government – had become electoral liabilities, led to her replacement by John Major in December 1990.

Major had been instrumental as Chancellor of the Exchequer in persuading Thatcher to take the UK into the ERM in October 1990, but apart from that was not perceived as having a defined profile on EC policy. His close ally (and first Chancellor of the Exchequer) Norman Lamont was perceived as a mild Euro-sceptic. This lack of profile changed quite quickly as the government acted to reverse a perceived marginalisation of Britain. The new Prime Minister proclaimed in March 1991 that Britain's place was 'at the heart of Europe'. It was no accident that he chose to make this pronouncement in Bonn. Much younger than Thatcher, he possessed neither her wartime memories nor her exaggerated view of Britain's importance. Germany, and more especially Chancellor Kohl, was now seen as the obvious partner in the shaping of the Community. To that end, Chris Patten, the then Chancellor of the Duchy of Lancaster (i.e. Minister without Portfolio), who many see as the originator of the policy, was dispatched frequently to Bonn to make clear in private just how far Britain was prepared to go to meet at least some of the aspirations of her EC partners. A key role was also played at that time by Ludger Eling, the representative of the Konrad Adenauer Foundation in London, who acted as the link to the Conservative leadership. Eling was also central to the decision by Chancellor Kohl to go to Edinburgh in May 1991 where he referred to Major as *'eine Glückssache für Europa!'*, a 'stroke of luck for Europe'.[24]

In public, however, the 'heart of Europe' rhetoric continued to co-exist with a persisting hostility to the central thrust of the two IGCs. At every point Prime Minister Major, whose political experience was garnered in the Whips' Office, showed himself determined to carry along the minority of the Conservative parliamentary party who continued to share Thatcher's views and he was rarely prepared to confront her legacy. At the Maastricht Summit in December 1991, Major was, with the help of Kohl, able to score some successes. The attempt to secure a generalised 'opt out' on Monetary Union had by then failed and the UK government had to settle for a UK 'opt out' which left room for a later opt in. The downside of this success was to rule out the City of London as a serious contender for the site of a future ECB. It had also been possible to secure an 'opt out' on the Social Chapter.

In the election campaign of April 1992, the TEU had largely enjoyed all-party support, with the only point of dispute being 'the opt out' on the

Social Chapter. The two heavyweights among the Euro-sceptics, Mrs Thatcher and former cabinet minister Norman Tebbitt, had left the House of Commons and the first two readings of the Maastricht Bill were passed with all-party support. The Euro-sceptics were at that point, a small if vocal minority. After the Danish referendum in June 1992 the government, fearful of a large Euro-sceptic revolt, postponed the third reading until after the Summer recess. The decision to postpone the third reading of the Maastricht Bill already caused grave disappointment in Bonn, but worse was to follow. In September 1992 Britain had to withdraw from the ERM in deeply humiliating circumstances. In the wake of the withdrawal itself, much British analysis focused on the role of the Bundesbank and its President, Helmut Schlesinger, with invidious comparisons being drawn between the readiness of the Bundesbank to support the franc, and its alleged undermining of sterling.

The events of the Summer of 1992 effectively undermined any chance that there might have been of creating a privileged British–German relationship. Emboldened by what they saw as Prime Ministerial weakness, the Euro-sceptics, while still a minority, exercised an increasing influence as the government's small majority declined and John Major was forced to make permanent tactical concessions in the style and content of his European policy. It is doubtful in any case if such a relationship could ever have been robust. It is difficult to see how a deep British–German relationship could have been compatible with the Franco–German relationship. Such a relationship would also have run counter to the British preference for forming alliances on a case-by-case basis, often with great tactical skill, rather than longer-term alliances. Moreover, while Britain and Germany have many overlapping interests, the imperatives of identity, which have made Germany a 'reflexive Europeanist' and Britain a defender of sovereignty, have produced deep divergences on European policy, which are difficult to overcome in an under-institutionalised relationship.

The last months of the Major government provided a number of examples which showed how British policy could degenerate into fruitless attempts to tie all other EU policy to a particular issue of importance in the UK, most notably the BSE crisis and the controversy over the social policy opt out (where Major's government threatened to hold up progress in the IGC because of its disappointment at the ECJ ruling on working hours, which it held to have undermined the scope of the opt out). While such tactics arguably worked for Mrs Thatcher on the budgetary issue in the mid-1980s, over-use produced diminishing returns for Major.

By contrast, the German preference for longer-term relationships relies on agreement on key long-term goals and on a political elite that will cleave to these goals even against adverse public opinion as on EMU. These are criteria which UK governments – in general tending to privilege flexibility on issues and responsiveness to public opinion – are inherently unlikely to satisfy, and it was a test that the Major government, through its irresolution, decisively failed in the Summer of 1992. It is a test, though, which the Blair government, elected in May 1997, addressed head-on.

This 'New' Labour government had an attitude towards Germany that was strikingly different from its Conservative predecessors. In opposition, Labour had been impressed with many features of the German economy and Germany was also a crucial reference point in Labour's debates about constitutional reform. In power, Labour was determined to avoid the isolation which had been so ruinous to Conservative policy. Tony Blair quickly established a good working relationship with Helmut Kohl and showed sufficient flexibility at the Amsterdam IGC to succeed not only in avoiding isolation but in becoming an influential player. The prospect of a Schröder-led government aroused keen anticipation in London and was seen as an opportunity to raise the UK to the level of a co-equal player with France and Germany in the EU. British views, which crystallised after a Prime Ministerial Strategy Meeting on Europe in May 1998, embraced the language of 'step-change' and 'strategic alliances' in Britain's relations with key member states in the EU. While France and Germany were both envisaged as key partners, the assumption was that a Schröder-led government would be a *demandeur* in terms of developing joint initiatives and would view the UK as a strategic partner. The task for the UK government was to identify key common projects, short of full membership on EMU.

British views were based on the assumption that Gerhard Schröder would, like Helmut Kohl, be the key player in German European policy. They were also influenced by the debate which was sparked by the publication of Peter Hort's article '*Wird die Europapolitik britischer?*' (is [German] European policy becoming more British?), published in the *Frankfurter Allgemeine Zeitung* on 30 October 1997. This article argued on the basis of seminar observations by Hans-Friedrich von Ploetz, State Secretary in the German Foreign Office and Joachim Bitterlich, Kohl's European and Foreign Policy Adviser, that British policy ideas on Europe were becoming more attractive. Specifically, he argued that a much more British 'bottom-line' view was going to be taken of budgetary contributions and that future German European policy would have to show specific benefits in relation to every new proposal. British expectations of immediate increased interest on the part of the German government in a strategic alliance were always unrealistic, given the centrality of EMU, the launch date of its third stage and the impregnable character of the Franco–German alliance. The France-focused preferences of Oskar Lafontaine and Joschka Fischer also acted strongly to hold back any plans Schröder, who was held to be close to the UK, might have had. If the hopes for a strategic alliance proved impossible to realise, relations improved greatly after the demise of Oskar Lafontaine. This was confirmed in the unprecedented joint paper Schröder published with Tony Blair on 8 June 1999. Entitled (in German[25]) 'The Way ahead for Europe's Social Democrats', the paper presented a case for modernising Social Democracy to adapt it to what are perceived to be the demands of the contemporary era – above all the competitive challenges of a globalising economy. While it reiterated (some) more or less traditionally Social Democratic values – fairness, social justice, liberty, equality of opportunity, solidarity and responsibility to others – the paper unambiguously and enthusiastically supported the market economy as the best framework in which to secure these values, and rejected with equal vigour the 'old' politics of interventionist Social Democracy as inadequate for the task.[26]

Although in the German context the Blair–Schröder paper was essentially about Schröder attempting to stamp his own image on the SPD,[27] the paper was more broadly, and quite explicitly directed at setting the agenda for Social Democracy across the (mostly Centre–Left-led) member states of the EU. 'The challenge', the paper suggested, 'is the definition and implementation of a new Social Democratic politics in Europe', and the paper's overall aim is 'to give impetus to modernisation': 'Let the politics of the Third Way and the *Neue Mitte* be Europe's new hope', as the paper rather pompously put it.[28]

A vital point in this context is how the Blair–Schröder paper played among the Centre–Left EU governments it sought to influence. While some, e.g. Austria and Sweden, were generally positive, one in particular – the Socialist-led Jospin government in France – was bluntly dismissive. Jospin's view, not unreasonably, was that a Sinatra-esque French Left would continue to do it its own way, and did not need to take lessons from its British and German counterparts. While much of this reaction can be explained in terms of the demands of managing a diverse governing coalition ranging from moderate centrists to Cohn-Bendit Greens and Communists, it does indicate a clear difference of emphasis in the understanding of late-1990s Social Democracy. French Social Democracy remains more interventionist, more statist than that of Labour under Blair and that which Schröder aspires to for the SPD. Characteristically, as was noted above, this was reflected in the Lafontaine era in close Franco–German cooperation in economic and monetary policy matters. The suggestion was that the traditional Franco–German diplomatic axis had thus been infused with a new social democratic policy content.[29]

Any such whiffs of a new, ideologically grounded quality of Franco–German cooperation were blown away both by Lafontaine's departure and by Schröder's coming out as a Blairite. The latter places the German government closer in economic policy terms to more reform-minded member-state governments from the UK, Spain and elsewhere. In this context, the relationship with the UK is perhaps less important in terms of realising strategic objectives than in transferring UK experience in embracing globalisation across to Germany. The Blair–Schröder paper – which launched a long-lasting controversy in the SPD and Germany more broadly – is clearly about embracing globalisation as a way of securing European competitiveness. Were this line of thinking to become more widely adopted the consequences for Germany's European policy – and for UK–German partnership – would be very wide ranging indeed. By the Autumn of 1999, though, a succession of electoral setbacks for the SPD at Länder level was beginning to raise questions about Schröder's ability to pursue policies based on the vision of the *Neue Mitte*.

Germany and its partners: towards a balance

The recasting of Germany's relations with its western neighbours alongside and as an integral element in its commitment to European integration has been an outstanding success. Not only was this recasting a precondition for the market access that Germany's postwar export-orientated economy needed, but it was central to both Germany's emergence as an effective political actor in Europe and the creation and consolidation of the EC. The very positive experience of Germany by its partners in these relationships also established the context for their acquiescence to German unity. For the first time a German state was encircled by friends.

Even more fundamentally, the partnerships with Germany's immediate neighbours have provided the mechanism through which they have been able to accept and absorb Germany's growing strength and influence. This is most obviously the case in relation to France. Throughout much of the history of this relationship the balance of adjustment had to be made by successive German governments, which recognised that the attainment of deeper European integration, the primary German milieu goal, could only be attained with France and on French terms. By the 1980s, the balance had become much more equal and France accepted much of Germany's institutional agenda and, even more fundamentally, adopted the exigencies of German monetary policy. Post-unity, the balance shifted even more pronouncedly in the German direction. France can still check German aspirations, e.g. on strengthening the powers of the European Parliament, and there is a strong sense in which the EMU project could constrain and is intended to constrain German power. What is remarkable, however, is the degree to which the Franco–German relationship has served to contain the tensions potentially occasioned by the changing power balance. Indeed, Kohl and Mitterrand set out to utilise these tensions by shaping a deeper form of European integration in a series of initiatives launching Monetary and Political Union. Only more recently, with a 'more British' style of policy on budget issues from the end of the Kohl era onwards, and a new closeness to the UK under Schröder, has this relationship come under sustained pressure.

In Section I, four faces of power were alluded to and it is instructive to read them off in relation to the Franco–German relationship. The basis of the Franco–German relationship has been the rejection by Germany of the projection of power in a straightforward realist mode and the relationship, its mechanisms, symbols and assumptions act as a visible guarantee to the French political elite that this will continue to define the relations between the two states. In the area of indirect institutional power, French fears of a too demanding/dominant Germany are assuaged by the continued use of the Franco–German relationship as the vehicle for joint *démarches*. Unintentional power is a category that has gained in importance as Germany has become more central. Since it is unintentional, it is less easy to address directly through the Franco–German relationship but here again, the relationship is important. The most potent example here would be the impact of the transmission of higher German interest rates, determined by the Bundesbank to deal with specific German circumstances post-unity, to other European economies. While the Franco–German relationship had no formal leverage on the independent Bundesbank, the dense elite contacts created through the relationship meant that there was a much wider understanding of the reasons for the Bundesbank policy and it was not instrumentalised into wider disillusionment. Perhaps even more strikingly when the franc, like the pound, came under heavy, and in the case of the pound, intolerable pressure, the Bundesbank was held in the British case to be unhelpful (and even by some as the prime cause), while in the French case it played a key role in helping France remain within the ERM.

The final face of power, whereby Germany is systemically empowered by the fit between the systems of governance in Germany and the EU, tends to favour Germany, given the nature of the highly centralised French state, whose institutional configuration does not mesh so easily with the EU governance system. The cumulative effect of the various faces of German power has shifted the balance of adjustment onto France. This places the French elite in an exposed position vis-à-vis the French population, which may not perceive the reasons for adjustment. The maintenance of the relationship therefore depends strongly on elites adopting a resolute attitude towards the realisation of common Franco–German milieu goals. This is a bargain which the French elites understand and have been prepared to cleave to – even, despite periodic strains, under the conditions of cohabitation. In terms of its impact on German European policy-making, the Franco–German relationship, in its function as 'spine', has conformed to the overall pattern of strengthening German strategic capacity in the EU, while at the same time exacerbating tactical weaknesses by reinforcing sectorisation and making the construction of tactical deals with other member states more difficult.

The Dutch case diverges interestingly from the Franco–German relationship. Neither partner had sought to thematise the bilateral relationship in strong symbolic terms, and at the level of economic integration the relationship had been a spectacular success requiring little managing. Even at a political level and despite deep popular mistrust of Germany in the Netherlands, the views of successive governments were sufficiently encouraging to European integration to carry a successful relationship. In the post-German unity context the relationship did suffer from a number of strains at the political level, which were accompanied by a continuing high level of popular suspicion. In that context, the two political elites, but principally the Dutch elite, sought to deepen the relationship through policy alignment and institutional deepening. In particular, this was an open-eyed reaction by the Dutch elite to what they saw as an increase in German power and a further shift in the balance of adjustment, e.g. in the joint military arrangements, but it also represented a clear recognition by the German government that this imposes on it an obligation to devote increased care and attention to the maintenance of the relationship if good relations with the Netherlands were to continue and the Netherlands were to continue as a reliable partner in the achievement of German milieu goals.

In the case of the UK, the attempt to form a strategic partnership was not successful. Such a partnership assumes that the two governments have sufficient autonomy from their domestic base to give a great deal of weight to the maintenance of the relationship with the strategic partner over time, not just on a case-by-case basis. It also assumes some agreement at a deep level on goals. These preconditions were simply lacking in the British–German relationship, where views on the desirable goals of European integration differed widely, despite frequent agreement on specific policies. The relationship, unlike those with France and the Netherlands, also lacked a sufficiently deep level of institutionalisation to carry the balance of adjustment and to work for longer term convergence. Finally, Britain's realist conceptions and the contested nature of European integration came together to preclude the UK as a stable, long-term strategic partner for a Germany which wishes to change the regional milieu in a more integrationist direction. The advent of the Blair government has, though, held out the prospect of significant change, at the very least leading to the UK acting as a less confrontational and more engaged actor and, more broadly with the election of the Schröder government, beginning to deepen and institutionalise partnership and develop common UK–German initiatives.

On balance, Germany's internal consensus on Europe and the mind-set of its political elite have allowed it to manage its relationship with its partners in a manner that has been enormously useful in the realisation of its strategic goals. This strategic success is clearly illustrated in case-study Chapters 4 and 5 on the 1996–97 IGC and EMU. However, while the German capacity for strategic partnership is likely to continue, the crucial lubricating element provided by German budgetary power, which has been very important in structuring relations with other (typically poorer) parts of the EU, is now under much more pressure. This is a theme raised to particular prominence by the prospect of eastern enlargement of the EU, which will require a significant recalibration of the Union's common policies and budget and has the potential to recast also German alliance strategies. These are themes addressed in the final case study in Chapter 6.

Notes

 1 J. Anderson and J. Goodman, 'Mars or Minerva? A United Germany in a Post-Cold War Europe', in R. O. Keohane, J. S. Nye and B. Hoffmann (eds), *After the Cold War: International Institutions and State Strategies in Europe, 1989–1991* (Cambridge, MA: Harvard University Press, 1993).
 2 H. Simonian, *The Privileged Partnership: Franco–German Relations in the European Community 1969–84* (Oxford: Oxford University Press, 1985).
 3 Paterson, 'Beyond Semi-Sovereignty', 168.
 4 W. Wallace, 'Germany as Europe's Leading Power', *The World Today* (1995).
 5 This was most evident in the Kohl era, underlying a rhetoric which permeated almost all of his European policy speeches. A notable example was his speech at the University of Leuven on 2 February 1996, where he linked it to François Mitterrand's statement to the European Parliament on 17 January 1995: 'Nationalism is war'. The force of this rhetoric is little understood in the UK. See I. Davidson, 'Beyond the Catcalls', *Financial Times*, 7 February 1996.
 6 J. Weiler, 'Fin de Siècle Europe', in R. Dehousse (ed.), *Europe after Maastricht: An ever Closer Union?* (Munich: Löbe, 1994).
 7 Cited in T. Kielinger, 'Anglo-German Relationships within Wider Partnerships', speech delivered at Royal United Services Institute/Stiftung Wissenschaft und Politik Conference, Ebenhausen, 28 June 1996, 10.
 8 H. Wallace, 'Foreign Policy. The Management of Distinctive Interests', in R. Morgan and C. Bray (eds), *Partners and Rivals in Western Europe* (London: 1986), 162.
 9 See the *Independent*, 4 December 1998.
10 Both quotes cited in J. Stephenson, 'Anniversaries, Memory and Neighbours. The German Question in Recent History', *German Politics*, 5 (1996), 50.
11 See M. van Traa, 'Wohlbekannt aber ungeliebt? Der deutsche Nachbar aus niederländischer Sicht', *Europa-Archiv* (1994), 495.
12 Piet Dankert, 'Ein vereinigtes Deutschland in einer sich wandelnden Welt aus niederländischer und westeuropäischer Sicht', unpublished speech, Evangelische Akademie Tutzing, 15 January 1996, 7.
13 Ibid., 13.
14 Though eventually, on British insistence, the Luxembourger Jacques Santer was appointed.
15 L. Jansen, *Bekend en onbemind. Het beeld van Duitsland en Duitsers onder jongeren van vijftien tot negentien jaar* (Den Haag: Instituut Clingendael, 1993).
16 van Traa, 'Wohlbekannt aber ungeliebt?', 493.
17 Quoted in J. Stephenson, 'Anniversaries, Memory and Neighbours', 50.
18 Though some unease did return during the Schröder Chancellorship regarding the way in which smaller states were consulted during the German Presidency in the first half of 1999 on major issues such as the Kosovo conflict.
19 On Britain, Germany and NATO, see K. Kaiser and J. Roper, *British-German Defence Cooperation: Partners within the Alliance* (London: Royal

Institute of International Affairs, 1988).
20 Paterson, 'Beyond Semi-Sovereignty', 176.
21 Quoted in *Die Zeit*, 8 March 1996.
22 Y. Klein, 'Obstructive or Promoting? British Views on German Unification 1989/90', *German Politics*, 5 (1996), 414.
23 Quoted in the *Spectator*, 14 July 1990.
24 H. Kohl, *Our Future in Europe* (Edinburgh/London: Europa Institute/Konrad Adenauer Foundation, 1991), 16.
25 The English version had the clumsier and more anodyne title: 'Europe: The Third Way/Die Neue Mitte'.
26 T. Blair and G. Schröder, 'Europe: The Third Way/Die Neue Mitte', *http://www.labour.org.uk/views/items/00000053.html* (1999).
27 Cf. C. Jeffery and V. Handl, 'Blair, Schröder and the Third Way'.
28 Ibid., 16.
29 E.g. *Independent*, 14 October 1999, *The Times*, 22 October 1999, *Guardian*, 23 October 1999, *Observer*, 1 November 1999, *Financial Times*, 10 November 1999.

4
The 1996–97 Intergovernmental Conference

The preceding chapters have examined how German diplomacy in the EU is shaped by the internal institutional arrangements of the German political system and by the potentials for alliance-building with other member states which arise from the Europeanised identity German elites seek to project. The book now moves on to an analysis of key areas of European integration which German diplomacy has prioritised since the mid-1990s. There are three,[1] and these form the subject matter of this and the next two chapters which explore how internal institutional arrangements and external alliance-building capacity have impacted on the pursuit of the priority goals of German European policy:

1. the reform of the TEU in the 1996–97 IGC;
2. the completion of EMU in accordance with the timetable and criteria established at Maastricht;
3. preparing the ground for EU eastern enlargement, both through commencement of accession negotiations, and more immediately through pre-enlargement reform of the EU budget and of currently high-cost common policies in the fields of agriculture and structural/cohesion funding.

Basic positions for the IGC

The German negotiating position for the IGC was open and fluid. Policy positions were not formally set out in the early stages of the negotiations in any great detail, in stark comparison, for example, to the 1996 White Paper of the UK government on the IGC, but rather in the framework of five broad aims, literally on less than two sides of A4 paper.[2] Summarised, these were as follows:

1 Closer coordination in the second pillar of CFSP, including the establishment of a unit for planning and analysis and a general secretariat to give CFSP a higher profile, a closer WEU–EU relationship, and a diminution of the unanimity rule in favour of limited application of QMV.[3]
2 Strengthened cooperation in the third pillar of JHA, including communitisation of visa, asylum, customs and immigration policies, and a fuller framework for police cooperation in combating terrorism, international organised crime and the drugs trade.
3 A fuller democratic 'anchoring' of the EU through a strengthening of the powers of the European Parliament and national parliaments and a fleshing out of the subsidiarity principle in a protocol to the treaty.
4 Institutional reform to enhance the Union's capacity for action (in particular in view of the next enlargement rounds) by extending majority voting in the Council of Ministers (ideally alongside a revised 'dual' majority rule taking into account not just voting weights in the Council, but also the population sizes of the member states), and by streamlining the organisation of the Presidency, the Commission and the European Parliament.
5 And the facilitation of 'flexible integration' through the introduction of a 'flexibility clause' capable of transcending individual member states' vetoes on new integration initiatives.

The central message of the German aims was entirely consistent with the strategic project of deepening the EU (the 'exaggerated multilateralism' noted in Chapter 1) and of shaping the regional milieu in a way conducive to German political practices: the extension of the *multilateral* decision-making procedures characteristic of the supranational EC pillar into the two intergovernmental pillars established at Maastricht; and the broader strengthening of the *supranational* elements of the EU 'constitution' through democratic 'anchoring' and institutional reform. These were essentially suggestions for the incremental development of the broader institutional and policy *aquis* which has been recast since the mid-1980s. The positive emphasis given to the notion of flexible integration was more of a new departure given the contingent and essentially last-minute acceptance of flexibility (in the form of the EMU and social policy opt-outs/ins) at Maastricht. However, subsequent experience of Danish and, in particular, British reluctance to accede to further agendas of deepening, together with the broader problems associated with deeper foreign policy integration in those member states with traditions of neutrality (Austria, Finland, Ireland, Sweden), lifted up flexibility to a more general level of acceptability. Flexibility was seen to provide a mechanism for continuing to press ahead, even if the geographical scope of the milieu in which Germany was to be engaged was less comprehensive and/or differentiated by policy area.

Just as the themes of the German proposals for the IGC were consistent with the established thrust of European policy diplomacy, so was the lack of detail attached to the proposals entirely characteristic of the Federal Government's approach to major integration issues. It was an approach focused in one sense on the possibilities of bargaining with other member states. The aim was to shape the agenda in a declaratory sense, rather than to set out concrete objectives. As one senior diplomat expressed it: 'As long as we get what we want in general terms, we don't haggle on the details.' Concrete proposals for formulations for amending the treaty text at an early stage in negotiation would have been anathema; the calculation was that broadly and vaguely expressed formulations of priorities had a better chance of making it through the bargaining process and into the treaty in a way more or less satisfactory to the Federal Government.

In a second sense, the generality of the IGC proposals was focused on the necessities of interaction in the internal policy formulation process. While a consensus existed among domestic policy actors on the broad thrust of integration policy, individual actors had the capacity to veto particular details of policy. The level of generality of the five aims for the IGC was consequently pitched also to appeal to the internal consensus and shape a purposive agenda capable of mobilising that consensus, while simultaneously seeking to avoid any concrete positions potentially subject to domestic veto points. The way this combination of generality and flexibility evolved internally and externally in the IGC negotiations is discussed in the following in line with the structure established in Chapters 2 and 3 of this book: first, domestic institutional structures; and second external alliance-building capacity. Interestingly, interactions between the internal and external arenas became unexpectedly complex with the election of new British and French governments during the final phases of the IGC negotiations. While the new Blair government in the UK loosened the framework for negotiation, that of Lionel Jospin in France complicated the agenda by explicitly importing EMU into the context of the IGC debates. This engaged the German Federal Government in last-minute changes of emphasis which, in order to keep EMU on track, deprivileged some of its IGC aims and allowed unexpected room for manoeuvre for domestic actors in trimming those aims.

Domestic policy formulation for the IGC

Domestic policy formulation for the IGC in Germany was highly inclusive.[4] The Foreign Office, as lead coordinating body on political issues, was – and, in view of the potential for domestic veto points, had to be – open to input from a wide range of domestic institutions. This in part reflected its own weaknesses in policy coordination in a Federal Government constitutionally structured to allow extensive departmental autonomy. Sectorisation was no less evident in the IGC deliberations than in routine EU business. This, to the displeasure of other member states, was reflected physically in the size of the German delegations to the regular (weekly/fortnightly) working meetings of the IGC, which discussed questions of detail between monthly meetings at the Foreign Minister level. At the working meetings, it was not unusual for Foreign Ministry representatives to be accompanied by those of, say, the Economics and Finance Ministries, as well as the two Länder representatives. (The role of the Länder is discussed further below.) The various ministerial representatives from the Federal Government were not averse to pursuing their 'house policies' notwithstanding the stated aims of the Federal Government as a whole. One example was the unilateral circulation of a policy paper by the Environment Ministry without the requisite approval of the Foreign Office. Another was the attitude of individual ministries to extending QMV in the Council, as reported rather sensationally in the *Spiegel* and *Wall Street Journal* in September 1996.[5] While the Federal Government as a whole was clearly committed to extending QMV, individual ministries, in a political adaptation of the St Florian Principle,[6] apparently did not favour extension in their fields of responsibility: Interior on internal security and asylum, Finance on taxation and Economics on small business regulation. The Minister for Agriculture, Jochen Borchert, was even said to have sought the reversal of QMV rules in agricultural policy.

Although Germany was ultimately to veto extension of QMV in some of the policy fields of concern to the federal ministries, it would be an exaggeration to describe the ministries' reticence on QMV as a purposeful 'Euro-sceptical brake'[7] on progress at the IGC. It was rather the typical jockeying for position which can always emerge in a Federal Government structure which – given the relatively low status of the Foreign Ministry – lacks effective day-to-day mechanisms of coordination. It may create a rather amateurish impression of German diplomacy, but it can be overcome, as Germany's partners in the EU illustrated at the

Dublin Summit in October 1996, by reference to the Federal Chancellor. Helmut Kohl's custom was to stay aloof from negotiation on matters of detail, but typically to retain the right and authority to intervene where it was deemed necessary. Faced with the concerns of other member states, Kohl, according to a Foreign Office source, was moved to intervene after Dublin and knock ministerial heads together at the end of 1996. Kohl's traditional capacity for imposing coordination of the otherwise fractious tendencies of the ministries is a point to which the discussion will return later in the context of the QMV vetoes surprisingly entered by Germany in the final stages of the IGC.

The party politics of the IGC debates were relatively uncontentious. The early high profile taken by the CDU/CSU Bundestag *Fraktion* in the so-called Schäuble–Lamers paper was not maintained. Arguably, the Bundestag *Fraktion* had done its job by raising a controversial issue which was close to Kohl's concerns – that of a 'core Europe' – in a way in which Kohl could maintain a healthy distance and allow the related and less controversially phrased idea of flexible integration and the 'flexibility clause' to emerge in more orthodox interaction with the French government (see p. 85). After the Schäuble–Lamers paper, the CDU/CSU *Fraktion* in Bonn was quiet and supportive. The FDP, which had initially voiced disquiet about the Schäuble–Lamers initiative – not least because it circumvented 'its' Foreign Office – was assuaged by the softer formulation of the core Europe idea in the government declaration which followed the coalition's victory in the 1994 Bundestag election. It too was quiet and supportive thereafter. Even the CSU in Bavaria did not seek to profile itself party-politically on the IGC issue. Edmund Stoiber's Euro-assertiveness was pursued primarily through the policy structures of the Länder, and in any case seemed to be focused elsewhere: on the stringent observance of the EMU convergence criteria and on the (financial) problems of reforming the CAP and the Structural Funds in the face of eastward enlargement (see further in Chapter 6).

On the opposition benches there were few real divergences of opinion. Initially unconvinced by the notion of hard core/flexible integration, the SPD and the Greens – the latter by now committed to positive engagement in the EU – had at least accepted the idea. On other matters, such as the process for nominating Commissioners, differences of detail existed,[8] but rarely moved towards questions of principle. The only potential area of principled disagreement with the governing coalition was on employment policy, where SPD and Greens argued – against the opposition of the Federal Government and the coalition parties – for the inclusion of a new chapter on employment policy in the TEU. The Federal Government did, in the end, accede to incorporation of elements of the employment agenda into the treaty, though this emerged rather more from compromise with the new French government under Jospin than from successful opposition pressure.

The Federal Government was faced by rather more concrete constraints from the Länder and their rights of co-decision in European policy-making under the new Article 23 of the Basic Law. These rights were interpreted to allow them full access to the IGC negotiations. Supported by a dedicated Standing Group of the European Ministers' Conference of the Länder, two Länder representatives were delegated to the regular working meetings at the IGC, one from Rhineland–Palatinate (a small, SPD-led Land) and one from Bavaria (large and Christian Democratic). The mandate of the two representatives were substantial Bundesrat resolutions on the IGC issued in March and December 1995 and November 1996, respectively. The first two resolutions presented a mixture of demands directly of concern to the Länder and others more generally focused on the further development of the Union. These ranged from the unattainable (e.g. the demand for a full competence catalogue clarifying the distribution of competences between the EU and the member states) to the pragmatic (e.g. the incremental enhancement of the powers of the Committee of the Regions). More generally, they in no substantial sense conflicted with the broader thrust of policy laid out in the Federal Government IGC aims. The latter resolution from November 1996 did, with its focus on employment policy; this though, unlike the others, was a majority rather than a unanimous resolution, and represented more the SPD's party-political mobilisation of its Bundesrat majority than a concerted Länder aim.[9]

Generally, the cooperation between the Foreign Office and the Länder in the IGC ran smoothly,[10] with a good proportion of the Länder demands being directly tabled by the German delegation,[11] or being presented in a way broadly acceptable to the Länder representatives (e.g. the proposal for attaching a subsidiarity protocol to the treaty rather than rewording the subsidiarity clause within the treaty[12]). In view of this experience of positive cooperation and, more broadly, the location of Länder demands within the wider German consensus on IGC aims, the Länder could not be said to have imposed particularly onerous constraints on the Foreign Office in the IGC negotiations. They were certainly less of a constraint than they had been at the previous IGC round which culminated at Maastricht, where they had demonstrated a capacity to bind the Federal Government to positions it had no real sympathy for.

The fuller influence of the Länder at Maastricht was in large part due to the credibility of their threat that they might veto the ratification of the TEU. This credibility was based on their capacity over a period of years prior to the Maastricht process to generate a series of crisp demands behind which all of the Länder were unequivocally ranged, and to issue with a united voice a succession of Bundesrat resolutions, each reacting with impressive speed to the changing emphases of the IGC negotiations.[13] These conditions did not exist in the 1996–97 IGC. As noted in Chapter 2, the capacity for disunity among the Länder on sensitive political issues in the wider development of the European integration process increased significantly in the 1990s. This was evident in the formulation of the first two Bundesrat resolutions on the IGC in March and December 1996. In the former, important differences over such matters as the future of the Committee of the Regions, which had come clearly to light in the European Ministers' Conference, were only patched into a common position for presentation by the Bundesrat with some difficulty.[14] And the formulation of the latter resolution was even more fraught. A compromise recommendation (stitched together from two competing drafts) was made by the Bundesrat EU Committee on 24 October 1995 for the Bundesrat to accept a proposal for a second resolution on the IGC. Some seventeen proposals for amendment[15] were then tabled between 23 November and 14 December 1995. Only a last-minute meeting behind closed doors on 15 December 1995 secured the necessary consensus for a final resolution to be passed unanimously (but not without elements of acrimony[16]). It is for this reason – the difficulty of building consensus – that the Länder were unable to issue the highly effective supplementary resolutions they deployed so purposefully in the previous IGC round. Indeed, the only 'supplementaries' issued in the last phases of the IGC were on extremely narrow concerns about the status and rights of broadcasting and banking institutions in the Länder.[17]

As Gerd Walther, European Minister in Schleswig-Holstein, put it in the Bundesrat in December 1995, the Länder could only manage this time to cobble together with some difficulty a unanimous voice; what they could not manage was *agreement*.[18] This was confirmed in the third main Bundesrat resolution of November 1996 in which a demand for a more purposeful EU employment policy was driven by the SPD majority in the Bundesrat and failed to secure consensus. In these circumstances, the prospect of a credible Länder veto threat over some especially cherished

IGC aim, e.g. subsidiarity or the establishment of the Committee of the Regions at Maastricht[19], was remote.

This, of course, was quite evident to the Federal Government. It may not, however, have been entirely evident to Germany's EU partners. In theory, this represented a negotiating tool for the Federal Government in the IGC negotiations. The Federal Government could claim to be bound externally, with reference to Article 23, by certain Länder demands in a situation where a Länder capacity to bind did not exist internally. Consequently, a high trade-off price could potentially be extracted for negotiating away the Länder demands which had been tabled, but without the Federal Government facing any real threat of internal sanction for doing so. This may well have explained the relatively open attitude of the Foreign Office to tabling Länder demands in the working meetings of the IGC.

It was therefore somewhat surprising that, in the final phase of negotiations in the IGC, Länder resistance was widely deemed to have been responsible for Chancellor Kohl vetoing the extension of QMV in areas such as environmental and industrial policy[20] (amid the considerable irony that the UK, hitherto the blocking power on extending QMV, was now, under Tony Blair's leadership, content to support the extension of QMV in these cases). While it was, on the surface, true that the Länder had played the veto card, there are two reasons why this should not be read as a renewed bout of Länder assertiveness such as that displayed at Maastricht. First, the Länder did not, as has been stressed, put up a potent united front in the IGC culminating at Amsterdam. Kohl could, in all likelihood, have faced them down or offered some internal concession to pay them off or split them. That he did not reflected the fact that their resistance to extension of QMV coincided with positions held by his own federal ministries; 'awarding' the Länder the responsibility for the vetoes deflected attention from a perhaps more embarrassing reality of fractiousness in his own government.

Even so, conceding to this alliance of opposition in the Länder and the federal ministries rather gave the lie to Kohl's reputation for being able to 'knock heads together' and ultimately graft together the conflicting positions of sectorised government into some form of final negotiating package. The reason for this – and the second reason why the Länder were successfully able to hold to a veto position – lay in the difficulties injected into the final phase of negotiation by the new Jospin government in France. Elected just a fortnight before the conclusion of the IGC at Amsterdam, Jospin's election manifesto had committed him to seek treaty changes in the field of employment policy, which were presented as a quid pro quo for adhering to previous Franco–German consensus on EMU. Given that the results of the IGC had in any case fallen far behind initial expectations of laying the institutional groundwork for eastern enlargement of the EU, Kohl privileged accommodation with the French to keep his holy grail of EMU on track and allowed – or did not have the time or energy to prevent – the German delegation to go 'off message' on QMV.

For once, then, in light of last-minute changes in external parameters, the internal constraints of sectorised ministerial government and the federal system, acted, as they were constitutionally designed to do, as a *Machtschranke*, a limit on the power of the head of government, and not, as they have tended to do in European policy-making (see Chapter 2) as an *Ermächtigung*, an empowerment, for the Chancellor, which had accorded Kohl in the past a certain leeway which could be brought to bear in interaction with the other member states. An equally unusual role reversal was revealed in the external partnership-building dimension of Germany's diplomacy in the IGC, with the UK taking over the mantle of friendly partner and France posing unexpected difficulties in the final IGC negotiations.

Relations with partners

France

The initial framework for Franco–German cooperation at the 1996–97 IGC was rather different than the previous IGC round which culminated at Maastricht. On the one hand, President Chirac's administration proved both to be somewhat more unpredictable and to be more open to a stance of national self-assertion than that of his predecessor, Mitterrand.[21] On the other, the agenda of the IGC was, initially at least, tilted rather more to the German side of the trade-off (deepening towards Political Union), which sustained the Maastricht negotiations than that of the French (progress towards EMU as a means of binding in unified Germany). With EMU officially bracketed out of the IGC discussions, the scope for a Franco–German package deal was narrowed (at least until the final stages of the negotiations, when, unofficially, EMU burst in prominently onto the agenda). As a result, significant differences emerged, particularly in issues relating to conceptions of national sovereignty.[22] Democratic 'anchoring' from the French perspective was seen much more in the sense of strengthening the role of national parliaments in European decision-making than that of the European Parliament, and a certain reticence also existed vis-à-vis the overtly integrationist stance of Germany in the two intergovernmental pillars of CFSP and JHA. Consequently, while there was general support on the French side for extending majority voting procedures in all three pillars, there was an attempt to retain the fall-back position of the Luxembourg Compromise for those situations where core national interests are felt to be at stake.

Nevertheless, there was a common concern to maintain the tradition of the Franco–German motor and to present where possible a joint position capable of transcending differences over particular issues. This was made possible in part by the progress, in parallel to the IGC, of important negotiations on EMU, in particular the discussion of a 'stability pact', informally enabling at least part of the Maastricht trade-off between EMU and Political Union to be maintained. In addition, both Kohl and Chirac and their respective Foreign Ministers Kinkel and de Charette sought to present common platforms, at least in an outline sense, on the major issues facing the IGC, for example:

- the Kohl–Chirac Joint Letter of 6 December 1995, which was more or less synonymous with the German Foreign Office's subsequent 'Aims for the IGC';
- the Kinkel/de Charette 'Guidelines for CFSP' of 27 February 1996;
- and the two Foreign Ministers' further proposals, agreed 'down to the last letter' on CFSP in March 1997.[23]

The Foreign Ministers also published a joint paper on 17 October 1996[24] to flesh out the notion of flexible integration flagged up in the Kohl–Chirac Letter. Flexibility – reclothed here as 'enhanced cooperation' – would give those member states which can agree on a deeper level of integration the freedom to press ahead as a vanguard group which others would – if they wished – be free to join later. Non-participants would not have the power to veto such initiatives. The accelerated momentum behind the flexibility idea in the latter part of 1996, which continued through to its recognition in the treaty concluded at Amsterdam, was explainable as a form of Franco–German unity in the face of the hostility to deeper cooperation presented by the Major government in the UK in its intractable anti-integration stance in the IGC. The prominence it took on in the IGC debates[25] reaffirmed the centrality of the Franco–German axis and created a general and concrete point of commonality around which differences over particular issues could be packaged and traded off. It pointed to what seemed likely to be the end-game of the IGC: Franco–German agreement over general principles of integration which would act as a facilitator for wider consensus (the UK, perhaps, excepted) in other, narrower areas.

Of course, the end-game proved to be rather different as a result of the elections held in Britain and France in May and June 1997, respectively. The election of the Labour government under Tony Blair overturned previous British obstructionism (see p. 68), while the Socialist-led government under Lionel Jospin had rather the reverse effect on the IGC negotiations. Elected not least because of public disillusionment at the high price in terms of unemployment and fiscal austerity paid in France as a result of the quest to meet the EMU convergence criteria, Jospin was obliged to seek some compensation for the French electorate from the IGC. This took the form of French pressure for the EU to adopt measures to promote employment, which was brought explicitly into connection with the Stability Pact for the policing of the economic convergence upon which EMU is based. Both the cost implications of an EU employment policy and the connection to the Stability Pact were highly unwelcome to the Kohl government, provoking in some eyes a 'crisis in Franco–German relations'.[26] While a compromise was struck at Amsterdam, with the Stability Pact formally agreed alongside a commitment to concert efforts in employment policy[27] and to review these in a 'jobs summit' late in 1997, the issue deflected attention at a crucial moment from the IGC agenda and condemned the IGC outcome to one more minimalist than might otherwise have been expected.

The Netherlands

The IGC did not, in reality, present any great test for the relaunched, and generally positive relations between Germany and the Netherlands after the departure of Ruud Lubbers. There were no significant differences over CFSP, JHA, the question of democratic 'anchoring' or the principle of flexibility,[28] despite the pressures from the VVD (Liberals) within the Dutch governing coalition for the adoption of a more sceptical policy stance.[29] The only potential problem area would seem to have been on institutional reform, where the Dutch position – supported in concert by Belgium and Luxembourg – was one keen to preserve the (over-) weighting of smaller states in QMV, the rotating Presidency and the principle of one Commissioner per member state.[30] This, of course, was not entirely consistent with the German position and posed a test for the German commitment, noted earlier in Chapter 3, to supplement the Franco–German core relationship with an additional outreach to the smaller states of the Union. On one occasion – a Franco–German declaration on their 'nearly identical views' on the IGC in January 1997 – the Dutch government publicly expressed its displeasure at the absence of this outreach in practice.[31] Against such opposition, the German delegation ultimately backed off from substantial reform of the over-weighting of small states, shelving the issue for when the 'time was riper'.[32] Otherwise, though, the potential for Dutch–German trade-off remained extensive given the proposed developments in other areas such as the institutional development of CFSP[33] in which the Dutch had long claimed an interest.

The UK

The hope of establishing an outreach to the UK, which fleetingly existed in the early period of John Major's Prime Ministership, proved to be a vain one as long as Major's government remained in power. However warm the personal relationship between Major and Kohl may have remained, there was little prospect of finding many points in common with the Conservative government in the IGC discussions. On one level, the points of orientation of the two governments on the IGC were fundamentally at odds, with senior diplomats from the two countries variously presenting the IGC as a '3,000 mile service' which would tie up a few loose ends left over by Maastricht and little else (the UK), and as a 'tremendously important' enterprise (Germany). The subsequent presentation of British viewpoints on the IGC saw no convergence, with the UK representative to the Reflection Group famously tabling fifty amendments the day before the Reflection Group report was published,[34] and the UK White Paper on the IGC offering little sense of movement on most of the core issues outlined as priorities in the German 'Aims for the IGC', including enhanced integration in CFSP and JHA, strengthening the European Parliament, more generally extending majority voting, and so on. The starkness of the differences prevented constructive interaction, even in those areas where some overlap existed (e.g. boosting the institutional presence of CFSP or streamlining the Commission). This was all the more so, given the way in which traditional German prejudices had been mobilised by elements within the Conservative Party as a rallying point for Euro-sceptical mobilisation around issues such as the BSE crisis, the Social Chapter and EMU.[35] Against this kind of background, the attempts by the Major government to impede EU business over BSE and the Social Chapter had the effect of hoisting the flexibility question towards the top of the IGC agenda. The sense of frustration which British obstructionism created within Germany and beyond lent wider momentum to the German idea that the 'slowest ship' should not determine the speed of the convoy. In this context, the notion of flexibility became one more or less explicitly directed, through the proposal that flexible integration initiatives should not be subject to veto by those not wishing to participate, at providing an institutional framework for British isolation.

The sense of the UK being a lost cause under Major's government was confirmed by the extremely positive reception Tony Blair and other leading members of the Labour Party had begun to receive in Germany and elsewhere in the EU.[36] Even though in core areas the Labour Party's views on the IGC, as published in opposition, differed only in tone and emphasis from those of the Major government, there was a more or less undisguised hope in Germany[37] that the 1997 UK election would deliver a change of government.

Such hopes, which acted as a pregnant testimony to the negligible scope for UK–German cooperation at the IGC prior to the UK election, were, of course, fulfilled by the Labour Party's landslide victory on 1 May 1997. Initial concerns that the 'competitive Euro-scepticism' that Labour had entered into as a tactic to neutralise Europe as an electoral issue[38] might translate into a revived 'awkward partnership' in the IGC rapidly proved to be unfounded. Even in its first week in government, Labour set out impressive credentials for a constructive engagement in the EU, including an explicit commitment to sign up to the Social Chapter, the positive atmosphere of the visit by the new Foreign Secretary, Robin Cook, to his French and German counterparts, and two steps designed to reveal a more positive attitude to EMU: the granting of operational independence to the Bank of England, and the appointment of Sir David Simon, then Chairman of BP and the UK's EMU-friendliest industrialist, to a junior ministerial position dealing with trade and competitiveness in the EU.

British constructive engagement under Blair was reflected clearly in the Amsterdam Summit itself. There emerged considerable scope for UK–German cooperation, not least in resolving the Franco–German 'crisis' over employment/EMU, with Blair siding with Kohl in heading off formal expenditure commitments under the employment heading, while backing Jospin over the need for (though not the type of) action in employment creation. One of the potential sticking points between the German and UK positions – over closer cooperation in JHA – was resolved with Blair winning the freedom to retain an independent UK border policy while simultaneously removing UK opposition to closer cooperation in JHA on the part of those member states – such as Germany – which sought such cooperation. A similar trade-off was made on the role of the WEU in future security cooperation, with the conclusion of a final position which accommodated both the UK preference for the pre-eminence of NATO and the German priority ultimately to move to the integration of the WEU into the EU framework. Ironically, given the previous Major government's commitment to oppose any extension of QMV, the UK delegation found itself in the slightly bemusing position of having been prepared to accept QMV in a range of policy areas where extension was ultimately vetoed by other member states, including, as noted earlier, Germany.

Notes

1 As outlined in the Joint Letter of Kohl and Chirac to the President of the European Council on 6 December 1995, as endorsed in the Agenda 2000 issued by the European Council in Madrid on 15/16 December 1995, and as reiterated in the German Foreign Office paper 'German Aims for the Intergovernmental Conference' of 26 March 1996.
2 As in 'Deutsche Ziele für die Regierungskonferenz', Auswärtiges Amt paper, 26 March 1996, and at similar length in the Kohl–Chirac Joint Letter of 6 December 1995, as reprinted in M. Jopp and O. Schmuck (eds), *Die Reform der Europäischen Union. Analysen – Positionen – Dokumente zur Regierungskonferenz 1996/97* (Bonn: Europa Union Verlag, 1996), 116–17.
3 Only in this area were more detailed aims formalised first in a series of 'Guidelines' on CFSP set out jointly by the Foreign and European Ministers of France and Germany on 27 February 1996, as reprinted in Jopp and Schmuck, *Die Reform der Europäischen Union*, 118–20, and subsequently in a series of (unusually concrete) formulations for the treaty text prior to the Dublin Summit in late 1996.
4 For an alternative, insider's view from the German Foreign Office of the IGC negotiations, see G. Birgelen, 'Europapolitische Meinungsbildung in Deutschland', in W. Weidenfeld (ed.), *Deutsche Europapolitik* (Bonn: Europa Union Verlag, 1998), 103–27.
5 'Kreuze beim Nein', *Der Spiegel*, No. 40, 30 September 1996; 'German Ministries Reject EU Majority Voting Concept', *Wall Street Journal Europe*, 30 September 1996.
6 Described as such, with a sense of resignation, by a German Foreign Office official. The traditional appeal of individuals to St Florian, the patron saint of firefighters, is thus: 'St Florian, verschon' mein Haus; zünd' andre an!' ('St Florian, spare my house; set someone else's on fire!').
7 'Kreuze beim Nein', *Der Spiegel*, No. 40, 30 September 1996.
8 With the SPD proposing at its 1995 party congress the election of Commissioners by the European Parliament rather than the current process of post-nomination scrutiny by the European Parliament. See Istituto Affari

Internazionali, *Revision of Maastricht. Implementation and Proposals for Reform. A Survey of National Views*, Fifth Bulletin (January–June 1996), 20.
9 W. Fischer, 'Von Maastricht nach Amsterdam. Die Regierungskonferenz aus Sicht der deutschen Länder', *Zeitschrift für Parlamentsfragen*, 29 (1998), 57.
10 See G. Blume and A. Graf von Rex, 'Weiterentwicklung der inhaltlichen und personellen Mitwirkung der Länder in Angelegenheiten der EU nach Maastricht', in F. Borkenhagen (ed.), *Europapolitik der deutschen Länder. Bilanz und Perspektiven nach dem Gipfel von Amsterdam* (Opladen: Leske und Budrich, 1998).
11 The only major exception being the Länder demand for rights of appeal of the Committee of the Regions (on subsidiarity issues) and regions whose competences are unduly infringed by European institutions (i.e. above all, themselves) to the European Court of Justice.
12 So K. Klär, Rheinland-Pfalz Plenipotentiary to the Federation and on Europe in *Der Bevollmächtigte des Landes Rheinland-Pfalz beim Bund und für Europa* (ed.), *Reformen für ein bürgernahes Europa. Die Regierungskonferenz 1996*, 2nd edn (Bonn: Rheinland-Pfalz, 1996), 19.
13 Jeffery, 'The Länder Strike Back', 7–9.
14 See C. Jeffery, 'The German Länder and the 1996 Intergovernmental Conference', *Regional and Federal Studies*, 5 (1995).
15 Covering matters ranging from subsidiarity, the Committee of the Regions, access to the Court of Justice, equal opportunities policy, environmental policy, sport, human rights, churches, the EU budget and agricultural policy. See Bundesrat, *Drucksachen* 667/2/95 through to 667/18/95. We are grateful to Matthias Mähring on this point.
16 Bundesrat, *Stenographischer Bericht* 692. Sitzung. 15 December 1995, 591–2.
17 Cf. Fischer, 'Von Maastricht nach Amsterdam', 58–9.
18 Bundesrat, *Stenographischer Bericht* 692. Sitzung. 15 December 1995, 591–2.
19 Jeffery, 'The Länder Strike Back', 11.
20 See e.g. *Guardian*, 3 October 1997.
21 Cf. A. Szukala and W. Wessels, 'The Franco–German Tandem', in G. Edwards and A. Pijpers (eds), *The Politics of European Treaty Reform. The 1996 Intergovernmental Conference and Beyond* (London: Pinter, 1997), 88–90.
22 O. Schmuck, 'Die EU-Regierungskonferenz 1996: Zum Stand der Reformdebatte', *Integration*, 18 April 1995, 71.
23 The former two initiatives are reprinted in Jopp and Schmuck, *Die Reform der Europäischen Union*, 115–20, the latter reported in the *Guardian*, 4 March 1997.
24 'Verstärkte Zusammenarbeit im Hinblick auf die weitere Vertiefung des europäischen Einigungswerks. Gemeinsamer deutsch-französischer Diskussionsbeitrag für die Regierungskonferenz', Bonn, 17 October 1996.
25 For Alexander Stubb, 'the single most important politico-institutional issue of the 1996 IGC'. Quoted in A. Stubb, 'The 1996 Intergovernmental Conference and the Management of Flexible Integration', *Journal of European Public Policy*, 4 (1997), 37.

26 *Guardian*, 16 June 1997.
27 Cf. J. Hesse and M. Schaad, 'Leapfrogging, Side-Stepping or Paradise Lost? Amsterdam and the European Union', *Staatswissenschaften und Staatspraxis*, 9 (1998), 129–31.
28 A. Pijpers and S. Vanhoonacker, 'The Position of the Benelux Countries', in G. Edwards and A. Pijpers (eds), *The Politics of European Treaty Reform*, 129–33.
29 Istituto Affari Internazionali, *Revision of Maastricht*. Fifth Bulletin (January–June 1996), 12.
30 Jopp and Schmuck, *Die Reform der Europäischen Union*, 163–8.
31 'The actions of France and Germany ... undermine the Dutch presidency and are characteristic of the crass way in which the larger member states within the European Union ignore the smaller ones. It is arrogant and it is not effective ... if Germany and France want to support the Dutch presidency we welcome it but this is a strange way of doing it.' So Frans Weisgals, Dutch foreign affairs spokesman, quoted in the *Guardian*, 21 January 1997.
32 According to a senior German source in October 1997.
33 Pijpers and Vanhoonacker, 'The Position of the Benelux Countries', 131–2.
34 C. Jeffery, 'Britische Positionen zur Regierungskonferenz 1996 – Ein Wandel in Sicht?', in *Maastricht II – Zum Erfolg verurteilt?* (Erfurt: Schriftenreihe des Thüringer Ministeriums für Justiz und Europaangelegenheiten, 1996), 32.
35 See J. Buller and C. Jeffery, 'Britain, Germany and the Deepening of Europe', in K. Larres and E. Meehan (eds), *Uneasy Allies: British–German Relations and European Integration Since 1945* (Oxford: Oxford University Press, 2000).
36 E.g. the Social Democratic heads of government in the EU (see the *Independent*, 3 March 1996), and in a number of side-meetings at the EU Summit in Dublin on 13–14 December 1996.
37 E.g. the controversy in the UK stirred up by Klaus Kinkel's comment in December 1996, expressed in the context of the next UK general election, that 'Europe needs Britain' (Quoted in the *Independent*, 31 December 1996). This could not be easily reconciled with a hope that the increasingly Euro-sceptical Major government would be re-elected.
38 Cf. W. Paterson and C. Jeffery, *Großbritannien nach dem Machtwechsel: New Labour, Devolution und Europapolitik* (St. Augustin: Konrad-Adenauer-Stiftung Arbeitspapiere, 1997), 10.

5
Economic and Monetary Union: understanding Germany's European diplomacy

Basic positions on EMU

Through to the launch of Economic and Monetary Union on 1 January 1999, EMU was *the* defining element in German European policy and its continuing aspiration to effect milieu change. It entailed (and entails) far more profound and long-term consequences than anything decided at the 1996–97 IGC.[1] It has also been the aspect of European policy where German unification most obviously acted as a spur to further integration. Two features of EMU policy-making are especially noteworthy. First, the positions presented by Germany were untypically closed and far less subject, from the German perspective, to negotiated trade-offs with other member states. EMU was therefore rather less representative of the broad thrust of German European diplomacy than the IGC. This reflected the nature of the internal decision-making process in which the Federal Government had to accommodate Bundesbank insistence – buttressed by the Constitutional Court's decision on the TEU and a suspicious public opinion – on 'exporting' a pattern of monetary policy governance modelled explicitly on that which obtains within Germany.

Second, this process of 'export' was actually welcomed by the monetary policy authorities of most other member states. This was already evident in the Committee of EC Central Bank Governors in their deliberations on the draft statute for a European Central Bank in the pre-Maastricht negotiations, where the governors, rather to the Bundesbank's surprise, 'were more than happy, indeed eager, to create a Bundesbank "writ large"', and thereby to 'borrow' credibility from the Bundesbank and the DM.[2] These favourable conditions for Bundesbank institutional export prevailed through the 1990s to EMU's launch, and are explored below in respect of domestic factors and external alliance-building capability.

Domestic policy formulation for EMU[3]

The character of EMU as a 'two-level' game between the domestic and European arenas, together with the centrality of the policy, ensured that the policy community involved remained by German standards fairly restricted. Policy was shaped by the Finance Ministry, the Economics Ministry, the Foreign Ministry, the Chancellor's Office and the Bundesbank. Despite sometimes contradictory positions in this policy community, with the Chancellor's Office and the Foreign Ministry normally pressing for faster progress and the Finance Ministry and the Bundesbank displaying characteristic caution, German policy-making in this area was strikingly effective in shaping the debate in accordance with German priorities. The Finance Ministry was the responsible ministry and was most continuously involved, with the Chancellor and the Chancellor's Office also playing major roles and making many of the crucial decisions, especially in relation to strategic issues like the overall political direction of Germany and Europe and the timing question, the latter because of its obvious electoral implications. The Foreign Ministry played a crucial role in launching the EMU project at the outset and remained involved because of the project's importance to the wider integration process. However, the coordination mechanisms for the negotiation of EMU established at Maastricht privileged the Finance Ministry and kept the Foreign Ministry to some extent at arm's length.

Throughout, EMU was a policy essentially handled at the federal level with only very restricted input from the Länder. While representatives of two Länder Finance Ministries were part of the Finance Ministry-led inter-ministerial coordination group which prepared the EMU negotiating positions for Maastricht, their role was not one which involved genuine *Mitwirkung*. Moreover, although the Länder took formal positions on EMU via a number of Bundesrat resolutions prior to Maastricht, these essentially backed up the Federal Government/Bundesbank negotiating platform and had no real negotiating value for the Länder (unlike their parallel resolutions on Political Union – see Chapter 2). On the debates on preparations for the implementation of Stage III, the Länder had no formal input, though some Länder voices – notably those of Bavarian Minister-President Edmund Stoiber and his Saxon counterpart Kurt Biedenkopf – argued forcefully that in no circumstances must the convergence criteria established at Maastricht be diluted, even if this should mean a delay in the EMU timetable.[4] One suspects in the case of Bavaria that this was one of the points over which internal CSU rivalry between the Federal Finance Minister (and CSU Chairman) Waigel and Stoiber was carried out.[5]

A crucial player in the EMU debates was the Bundesbank. While formally it had only a technical advisory role in EMU negotiations, its status as a central player in the management of German monetary policy, its considerable political resources – buttressed by its public standing – and its role in the EC Monetary Committee and the Committee of EC Central Bank Governors accorded it a more co-equal status. It had, of course, close links to the European Monetary Institute in Frankfurt where former Bundesbank officials like Peter Schlüter played key roles. The relationship of the Bundesbank with the Federal Government in this area as in others was one of shared responsibility and the Federal Government was at pains to co-opt the Bundesbank into the process, beginning with participation in the Delors Committee. This co-option was not always straightforward. The Bundesbank displayed a general tone of suspicion and scepticism about EMU from the foundation of the Delors Committee and persistently sought to ensure that the form of rules which have shaped its approach to monetary policy within the Federal Republic were 'exported' to the governance of EMU. It had considerable success in this, most notably in the Maastricht convergence criteria and rules on central bank independence, and in the symbolic location of the European Monetary Institute in Frankfurt. It remained, though, sceptical about the political will in the EU to adhere to the letter of the convergence criteria, and maintained pressure for the export of its own institutional standards via a strict reading of the criteria and the adoption of tough flanking measures, such as the proposals for a Stability Pact which emerged in 1996. The Stability Pact proposals were designed to ensure a persistence of monetary stringency capable of outliving the 'dash for the criteria' and the attempts to fudge accounting standards which characterised the EMU debate from 1996 to 1998 (not least in Germany itself[6]). This tough line was all the more convincing – and binding on the Federal Government – given that it accorded both with wider public concerns about the credibility of post-EMU monetary policy in the EU and the tenor of the FCC's position on EMU.

There was little doubt about the lack of enthusiasm of the German public for the move towards a single currency, with only around a third of the German electorate consistently favouring such a move over the period since 1977.[7] Even in mid-1998, shortly before the implementation of Stage III, only 28 per cent of Germans were for a united currency, with 44 per cent against.[8] It could indeed be argued that this scepticism was more securely anchored than in the UK where it remains embedded more in a rather diffuse set of attitudes about sovereignty than any specific attachment to the pound sterling. In Germany, by contrast, pride in the DM was and is very high.[9] Moreover, while the pound has typically lost value through periodic devaluations, the DM has remained one of Europe's hardest currencies; public opinion surveys revealed in this respect strong concerns that the Euro would perform much less well than the DM.[10]

This pattern of public opinion helps explain a number of key developments in the unfolding EMU debate: why the Federal Government had to insist on Frankfurt as the site for the ECB; why the Schäuble–Lamers paper purposefully left out Italy (perceived as a threat to the stability of the Euro) as a prospective member of the 'hard core'; and why a Stability Pact was felt to be necessary. It also helps explain why the Federal Government was so successful in securing its goals in this area since partner states recognised the tightness of the internal constraints which it faced.

The existence of public distrust of EMU ensured that, despite an overall party consensus on Maastricht (with the exception at the time of the Greens), a number of parties were tempted to instrumentalise EMU as an issue. In the case of extreme parties like the Party of Democratic Socialism (PDS) and the *Republikaner* and unknown categories like Manfred Brunner's *Bund Freier Bürger*, this occurred without wider resonance given the lack of public trust in these parties. The position of the SPD was, however, more crucial. While its policy stance was generally supportive of the EMU project, it periodically dipped its toes in the waters of EMU-scepticism. Oskar Lafontaine, then Minister-President of the Saarland, raised the issue in the last weeks of the 1994 federal election, but found little support at the time. And in the wake of the SPD's disastrous performance in the Berlin election of 22 October 1995, Rudolf Scharping, the then party leader, and Gerhard Schröder, then Minister-President of Lower Saxony and SPD Federal Economics Spokesperson, expressed strong doubts about the viability of proceeding to a single currency along with their intention of making the issue a central feature of the October 1998 Bundestag election. However, after serious internal and external criticism, the SPD at the national level reverted to a position of continuing support for the single currency, albeit flanked by an even greater stress on the necessity for the convergence criteria being met.

A crucial importance, therefore, resided in the decision by Dieter Spöri, the SPD leader in Baden-Württemberg, to contest the crucial Land election of March 1996 on the basis of a critique of the EMU and a call for the postponement of the single currency.[11] This campaign proved a resounding failure and the SPD actually lost 4.3 per cent in electoral support. There appeared to be four key reasons for the SPD's failure successfully to mobilise anxieties about the Euro. First, the SPD's policy in Baden-Württemberg was not shared by its trade union allies. Second, the SPD was not trusted on money matters and even those who were unenthusiastic about the transition to a single currency had a higher trust in the capacity of the CDU/CSU to manage the transition than the SPD. Third, trust in Chancellor Kohl in European matters remained very high. And fourth, the EMU issue did not seem to be electorally salient. Only a minority of Germans appeared at the time to believe that the Euro was imminent.[12]

The SPD failure in Baden-Württemberg to mobilise public opinion against EMU[13] was seen by Chancellor Kohl 'as having given us a clear mandate to pursue our policies'.[14] Baden-Württemberg thus marked a 'crucial turning point in the German domestic debate on EMU',[15] making it unlikely that the issue of postponing EMU would resurface in 1998, either in the federal election scheduled for September of that year, or, more immediately, in the Bundestag debate which would be needed on German entry (which ultimately took place in April 1998). Nor was it likely that a no-vote would emerge in the Bundesrat, even though the SPD had a blocking majority and two of the more independent-minded Christian Democratic Länder – Bavaria and Saxony – had raised the issue of delay.

Rather more significant in its influence over the EMU debate than the political parties was the FCC. The FCC has come to play an increasing role in integration issues and in its judgment on the constitutionality of the Maastricht Treaty on 12 October 1993, it laid down a number of important markers. The judgment clearly privileged legitimation of the move to EMU at the national level in its broader argument that the absence of a European *Staatsvolk* sets limits to the legitimising role of the European Parliament. On EMU more specifically, it established that the Bundestag had to rule on whether the convergence criteria had been satisfied before a move to the final stage. It also established that the test of Monetary Union is as a *Stabilitätszone* and that if EMU did not provide such stability then Germany could withdraw. This tough line – which broadly accorded with that of the Bundesbank and of the wider public mood – was reinforced by subsequent comments on the attainment of the Maastricht convergence criteria. In a speech in Bonn in October 1996, Paul Kirchhof, FCC Justice, maintained that the Court would have to consider constitutional complaints about a German decision to join EMU if it could plausibly be argued that the terms of the TEU had not been adhered to. This reflected the broad thrust of the October 1993 ruling which stated that only actions legitimately taken on a clearly ratified treaty basis would be valid in Germany. Moreover, Justice Kirchhof implied that if the Court were asked to judge on the validity of a decision to take the Federal Republic into EMU, it would consider 'only numbers' and not the wider political factors at play in the EMU debates. This was interpreted as clear-cut opposition to any fudging of the criteria in the case of Germany, where forecasts had become increasingly pessimistic about the prospects of meeting the 3 per cent public deficit criterion.

These widely publicised views gave succour to the stated intentions of a number of prominent German economists, including Professor Wilhelm Nölling, former member of the Bundesbank board, to take the issue to the FCC if the convergence criteria were weakened. The result was a 300 page complaint lodged by Nölling and three other university professors – Joachim Stabbaty, Wilhelm Hankel and Karl-Albrecht Schachtschneider – with the FCC on 12 January 1998. Their argument was that the introduction of the Euro would compromise what they referred to as 'the civil right to stability', a right they claimed is conferred on the German citizen by the Basic Law. They alleged that this right would be infringed by a decision that Germany would enter EMU even if the convergence criteria determined at Maastricht had not been met. The fact that Germany in 1997 had just met the 3 per cent target for the government deficit as a ratio of Gross Domestic Product (GDP) severely weakened the force of the argument. In a decisive judgment, the Second Chamber of the FCC unanimously rejected the complaint on 2 April. It ruled that, given that the Maastricht Treaty had already been accepted by the FCC as compatible with the Basic Law, there was no case against the government, assuming Bundestag approval. It also rejected the plaintiffs' plea for a delay in the start of EMU.

The continuing discussion of the constitutional issues surrounding EMU inevitably strengthened the role of the Bundesbank in interpreting the convergence criteria and in setting the parameters for the approaching parliamentary decision on EMU. While the Bundesbank Central Council encompassed divergent views on EMU, including marked scepticism, it was never likely that it would directly challenge what it viewed ultimately as a political decision. The Bundesbank President Hans Tietmeyer, was on record as saying he would never 'stab the Chancellor in the back' on the issue. The Bundesbank report on EU-wide progress in meeting the Maastricht criteria, published on 26 March 1998, was thus a key hurdle but always one likely to be surmounted.

The report was a sombre document which made clear Bundesbank reservations. Crucially however, it reached the judgement that the inclusion of all eleven countries nominated by the Commission could be justified on financial stability grounds although further measures would have to be undertaken. The bulk of the document pointed to shortcomings in the area of budgetary consolidation (including in Germany), the high debt:GDP ratio of Belgium and Italy, and the pressing need for labour market and social security reform if EMU was to be sustainable. The final paragraph makes it clear however that the decision is a political one. Thus, protected by a favourable decision from the Bundesbank, the Cabinet decision to proceed on 27 March was a formality. Finance Minister Theo Waigel presented it as a decision for the export of the German stability model (though one which still called for further measures to accelerate debt reduction and tighten budgetary discipline among EMU participants).

The final Bundestag debate took place on 23 April. Having surmounted the obstacles presented by the FCC and Bundesbank and inflicted defeat on the SPD when they attempted to use the EMU issue in the Baden-Württemberg election, Chancellor Kohl was in an enormously strong position. The move to Stage III was accordingly approved by an overwhelming majority of 575 votes to 35 with 5 abstentions (4 SPD, 1 CDU). Only the successors to the East German Communists, the PDS, voted against. Bundesrat endorsement was not, strictly speaking, necessary for ratification, but a defeat here would have been a serious setback. In the end though, only Saxony abstained. Its Minister-President, Kurt Biedenkopf, a long-time critic of Kohl used the debate to air East German concerns. The tactical nature of Bavarian opposition to moving to the third stage, as voiced by Minister-President Edmund Stoiber, was indicated by the manner in which he used the guardedly favourable verdict of the Bundesbank report to justify his positive vote despite his earlier critical rhetoric.

This discussion has confirmed a recurrent theme in this book, that domestic constraints can facilitate the achievement of milieu goals, in this case the establishment of an environment for monetary stability in EMU equivalent to that which exists domestically. Seen in this perspective, the impact of the FCC, the Bundesbank, those domestic voices calling for caution and delay and, indeed, wider public opinion trends was ambivalent. While they may complicate the decision-making process for the Federal Government, equally they may – simultaneously – actually have increased its leverage at the European level. The conditions set by the Bundesbank were seen as less negotiable by Germany's partners than if they had been the position of the Federal Government alone. This was all the more so, given the constitutional parameters set by the FCC around the EMU debate. Germany, it should be recalled, could not ratify the TEU until November 1993 due to the need to wait for the FCC's adjudication. The possibility of such a delay to the launching of EMU – which existed through to the FCC's EMU decision on 2 April 1998 – was a stringent discipline: definitely the Maastricht timetable and conceivably the entire EMU project could have been scuppered. This was not a palatable prospect for at least some of Germany's partners.

Relations with partners

France

The success of German policy on EMU was, therefore, clearly crucially dependent on external support. This external support cut two ways in what was a classic two-level game.[16] The commitment of the French government to EMU was used by Chancellor Kohl after 1989 as an argument that Germany must agree to EMU in order to demonstrate its continuing European vocation, but equally, as we have seen, the existence of domestic constraints could be instrumentalised by the Federal Government. The invocation of the Bundesbank was an especially powerful card here since Bundesbank positions – reflecting its status as independent central bank – were seen as containing little 'slack'.

Progress on EMU relied from the end of the 1980s on its uncontested status as *the* Franco–German project. It was also indicative of change in the balance of adjustment between the two partners. While French governments adopted German monetary policies after the collapse of Mitterrand's reflation policy, the EMU project offered the prospect of Europeanising the locus of monetary policy, a policy option which was held to be of particular interest to French governments. EMU then became the defining element and the touchstone of Franco–German relations after German unity, the very symbol of *Einbindung*. The Franco–German relationship set the agenda for all the crucial EMU negotiations, including Franco–German bilaterals pre-Maastricht. The relationship was also able to handle the crisis in 1992–93 when it looked as if the franc might have to leave the ERM, by pushing for a widening of the ERM exchange rate fluctuation bands.

In the run up to the decision to move to Stage III of EMU, the stakes were raised yet higher. Chancellor Kohl had vested his considerable political prestige in the project and both governments undertook considerable budgetary efforts to meet the convergence criteria. The French government's move to lower its budget deficit in 1997 by transferring 37.5 billion francs from France Telecom to the Treasury in return for its taking over future pension liabilities was criticised by officials from the Bundesbank and the Federal Statistical Office but accepted by the Federal Government. Kohl's government was more concerned by the action of Giscard d'Estaing in launching a debate on devaluation, which it feared might prove contagious and imperil the resolve of the French government. If this had proved to be the case, it would have had incalculable effects on German opinion and opened up a conflict of interests which even the institutionalised relationship might have struggled to overcome.

The devaluation question reaffirmed, though, a rather different approach to monetary policy in France than in Germany, one which is more comfortable with trimming inflation aims in the pursuit of other objectives, notably employment. This difference in approach was reflected in the debates on the Stability Pact, especially after the election of a Socialist government in 1997 committed to employment goals.[17] The Stability Pact was Germany's attempt to perpetuate the budgetary discipline throughout the EU shown in the run-up to Stage III *after* the launch of EMU, not least through an automatic procedure for 'fining' breaches. This pact did not mesh ideally with the 'monetary culture on the other side of the Rhine',[18] namely French concerns to establish a 'Stability Council' which might act as a 'political' counterbalance to the sheer and, no doubt at times uncomfortable, rigour of a Bundesbank-inspired monetary regime for EMU.[19]

Although Franco–German differences over the Stability Pact were papered over at Amsterdam, the underlying differences on how far a *gouvernement économique* was needed to supervise the functions of the ECB have remained live. They were certainly an underlying issue in the dispute in mid-1998 between Kohl and Chirac over the inaugural Presidency of the ECB, with Chirac putting forward Jean-Claude Trichet, then President of the French Central Bank, in opposition to Wim Duisenberg, in effect the German/Bundesbank nominee, but also the generally accepted candidate.[20] Though Trichet was generally acknowledged to be as tough a central banker as Duisenberg, Chirac's move was nonetheless seen as an 'attempt to secure possibilities of political influence on European monetary policy for Paris'.[21]

The more interventionist French stance briefly found a more positive resonance during the Lafontaine interregnum after the German change of government in 1998. Lafontaine quickly developed a close working relationship with the French Finance Minister, Dominique Strauss-Kahn, based on a common commitment to economic interventionism: 'markets need the regulatory hand of the state'.[22] Making use of the platform given by the expanded EU policy role of the Finance Ministry after the change of government in 1998, Lafontaine sought to establish an explicit link between the EU's (for him underdeveloped) employment policy and the (for him over-strict) monetary policy regime surrounding EMU. He implied that government expenditures on 'effective' employment programmes should be exempt from the strictures of the Stability Pact and that the ECB should hold down interest rates to stimulate demand and employment.[23]

This departure from the German postwar tradition of central bank independence in monetary policy lasted, however, only as long as Lafontaine, with Schröder reasserting the traditional position[24] after Lafontaine's resignation and implicitly underpinning it by propagating his anti-interventionist 'third way' agenda (see Chapter 3). Disappointed French complaints voiced later in 1999 that Germany after Lafontaine was no longer so interested in employment policy suggest that Franco–German differences persist and will remain an underlying tension as the EMU regime beds in.

The Netherlands
The Netherlands was closely aligned with the Federal Republic throughout on EMU. Although there was an initial divergence on the siting of the future ECB, the Netherlands remained the Federal Government's only consistent external supporter in its conception of the Stability Pact, expressing strong concerns in particular about Italy. This pattern of cooperation and common interest was reinforced by Germany's support for Wim Duisenberg (former President of the Dutch Central Bank and formally nominated by the Netherlands for the ECB Presidency) in the dispute with France over the Presidency of the ECB. This 'German–Dutch school around the axis of an independent Central Bank'[25] seems set to continue once EMU is in operation.

The UK
The UK has never been an ally on EMU, about which it has harboured strong reservations from the outset. The rival UK plan of the 'hard Ecu', presented to and dismissed by the pre-Maastricht IGC on EMU, proved to have very little attraction for other member states. The Federal

Government believed that it had subsequently neutralised opposition from the UK by helping secure it an 'opt-out', with a possibility to opt in later, at Maastricht. In the event, the decision of the Major government to continue to be involved in the preparations imported turbulence into the process. This was especially evident when it appeared the first wave of EMU might be rather narrow and that problems would arise between the 'ins' and 'outs', with the UK taking on de facto leadership of the 'outs'. However, on this issue unanimity is not necessary at the European level and the UK could ultimately not impede the move to EMU, especially since the number of 'outs' – four – turned out to be rather fewer than initially expected.

Moreover, with the election of the Blair government, the UK position changed to one of a commitment to join EMU in principle once a number of preconditions had been fulfilled (notably a convergence in economic cycles between the UK and EMU-Europe). While ruling out joining in in the first wave, the Blair government nevertheless moved into the role of facilitator. This facilitative and more positive attitude was of some importance given the UK's incumbency of the EU Presidency in the vital first months of 1998 when decisions on membership of the Euro-zone were taken. The quid pro quo has been a more accommodating position from Germany on keeping open channels of influence for the UK into Euro-zone decision-making. An important factor here has been the Blair government's zealous conversion to the merits of independent central banking, which stand to strengthen the German (and Dutch) stance rather than that of France on prioritising inflation goals.

Notes

1 C.f. the interview with Ralf Dahrendorf, 'Tanzen nach der deutschen Pfeife', *Die Zeit*, 31 May 1996.
2 Quoted in K. Dyson and K. Featherstone, 'EMU and Economic Governance in Germany', *German Politics*, 5 (1996), 341–2.
3 This section has benefited from the excellent analysis in Dyson and Featherstone, 'EMU and Economic Governance in Germany'.
4 *Süddeutsche Zeitung*, 8 May 1996; *Passauer Neue Presse*, 4 July 1996; *Guardian*, 16 June 1997.
5 See *Handelsblatt*, 15 January 1996 for a perspective on opinion inside the CSU.
6 See J. Janning, 'Bundesrepublik Deutschland', in W. Weidenfeld and W. Wessels (eds), *Jahrbuch der Europäischen Integration 1997/98* (Bonn: Europa Union Verlag, 1999), 311–12.
7 Bulmer and Paterson, *The Federal Republic of Germany and the European*

Community, 116.
8 So an Allensbach poll reported in E. Noelle-Neumann and T. Petersen, 'Die öffentliche Meinung', in W. Weidenfeld and W. Wessels (eds), *Jahrbuch der Europäischen Integration 1997/98* (Bonn: Europa Union Verlag, 1999), 297.
9 Allensbach Poll for the Bundespresse- und Informationsamt for the second half of October 1995, cited in W. Gibowski, 'Meinungen und Einstellungen der Deutschen zu Europa', unpublished speech, Weimar 24 October 1996. Eighty-four per cent of respondents expressed pride in the DM.
10 Cf. Noelle-Neumann and Petersen, 'Die öffentliche Meinung', p. 298.
11 See N. Reinhardt, 'A Turning Point in the German EMU Debate: The Baden-Württemberg Regional Election of March 1996', *German Politics*, 6 (1997).
12 W. Gibowski, 'Meinungen und Einstellungen der Deutschen zu Europa', 15.
13 The pattern was repeated in an 'EMU-sceptical' campaign in the Land election in Hamburg in September 1997, when the SPD's disappointing result led to the resignation of Oberbürgermeister Henning Voscherau.
14 Quoted in *Frankfurter Allgemeine Zeitung*, 26 March 1996.
15 Reinhardt, 'A Turning Point in the German EMU Debate', p. 93.
16 R. Putnam, 'Diplomacy and Domestic Politics: The Logic of Two Level Games', *International Organisation*, 42 (1989).
17 E.g. that of the respective Finance Ministers and central bankers on a 'stability council' in March 1996 (see 'Single Currency to be Policed by "Stability Council"', *Independent*, 27 February 1996), and the Joint Letter of Kohl and Chirac presented to the Dublin Summit of December 1996.
18 F. de la Serre and C. Lequesne, 'Frankreich', in W. Weidenfeld and W. Wessels (eds), *Jahrbuch der Europäischen Integration 1996/97* (Bonn: Europa Union Verlag, 1998), 318.
19 J. Janning, 'Bundesrepublik Deutschland', in Weidenfeld and Wessels (eds), *Jahrbuch der Europäischen Integration 1996/97*, 298.
20 Resolved in a classic fudge, with Trichet taking over at a point halfway through Duisenberg's term when Duisenberg would 'voluntarily' withdraw. Cf. F. de la Serre and C. Lequesne, 'Frankreich', in Weidenfeld and Wessels (eds), *Jahrbuch der Europäischen Integration 1997/98*, 334.
21 A. Pijpers and J. Rood, 'Niederlande', in Weidenfeld and Wessels (eds), *Jahrbuch der Europäischen Integration 1997/98*, 357.
22 O. Lafontaine and D. Strauss-Kahn, 'Europa – sozial und stark. Märkte brauchen die ordnende Hand des Staates', *Die Zeit*, No. 3 (1999).
23 Cf. O. Lafontaine, 'Notwendig ist Steuergerechtigkeit', *Das Parlament*, 27 November 1998, 8.
24 As reflected in the position set out (with regard to Lafontaine) in his initial government declaration: 'Nobody – I repeat: nobody – has called the independence of the Bundesbank and the European Central Bank into question.' Quoted in Regierungserklärung, 913.
25 A. Pijpers and J. Rood, 'Niederlande', in Weidenfeld and Wessels (eds), *Jahrbuch der Europäischen Integration 1997/98*, 357.

6
Eastern enlargement

Basic positions on enlargement

The question of enlarging the EU eastwards was an inevitable by-product of the end of the Cold War. For the post-Communist states of Central and Eastern Europe (CEE) their 'return' to a Europe of liberal democracy and market capitalism was indissolubly linked with the question of EU membership. Within the EU, there also emerged a strong (though not uniformly enthusiastic) commitment to open up a membership perspective for the post-Communist states as part of a wider strategy to embed a 'stable peace'[1] for the post-Cold War era. The result of these intersecting pressures has been a slow-burning, incremental enlargement process whose key stages have been:

- the conclusion of 'Europe Agreements' in December 1991, which awarded associated status and a (mainly) preferential trading relationship with the EU to Czechoslovakia, Hungary and Poland;[2]
- the Copenhagen European Council of June 1993 formally recognised the principle of (eventual) accession for the first time, while also initiating a permanent 'structured' relationship with the associated states;
- the Essen European Council of December 1994 set out a 'pre-accession' strategy for the associated states;
- in its 'Agenda 2000' of July 1997, the European Commission produced a series of proposals for reform of EU policies and the EU budget which enlargement would necessitate, together with comments on formal applications for EU membership tabled by ten CEE applicants;
- the latter provided the basis on which formal accession negotiations were opened in March 1998 with the Czech Republic, Estonia, Hungary, Poland and Slovenia (together with Cyprus);
- the Agenda 2000 package of policy reform and budgetary adjustment

was agreed during the German Presidency of the EU at the Berlin Summit in March 1999;
• reflecting the manifold technical and political difficulties involved in extending the *acquis communautaire* eastwards, accession itself is likely at the earliest around 2004, and more probably somewhat later.

Eastern enlargement has been and remains, in other words, a protracted political process. It has also been a process in which Germany, 'for a variety of reasons' has had 'a vital interest'.[3] There has certainly been a strong underlying moral commitment to enlargement (especially in the Kohl–Genscher era) rooted in Germany's co-responsibility for the Cold War and Europe's division. More recently, the concrete economic benefits German industry is drawing and will draw out of eastern markets have become increasingly important. Most fundamental throughout, though, has been an interest in enlargement as an instrument for stabilising the zone of transition to Germany's east, and therefore as a guarantor of German security. This security imperative has been the prime factor which has led Germany, from the early 1990s onwards, to pursue what might be termed the 'western integration' of its eastern neighbours.

The pursuit of this fundamental security interest has meshed with the CEE countries' own aspirations to EU membership to cast Germany as their advocate and their bridge into the EU. The pivotal role Germany has consequently assumed in the enlargement process has not always been easy to perform alongside existing commitments in the West, producing what Henning Tewes has termed 'role conflicts'.[4] The attempt to balance out the traditional role as 'integration deepener' with the new one of 'integration widener' has been a persistent feature of German enlargement diplomacy. It has also placed additional burdens of adjustment on the French side of the Franco–German relationship. This is all the more the case since the German policy of stabilisation/security is essentially one of extending the geographical reach of EU-Europe's regional milieu to Germany's eastern 'near-abroad' rather than to the Mediterranean south where the centre of gravity of French influence and interest lies. Eastern enlargement is, in other words, quite explicitly a 'milieu goal' aimed at 'shaping conditions beyond national boundaries' in Germany's interest. This is a point to which the discussion returns below.

It would be wrong to assume, though, that such a clear sense of Germany's interests in EU eastern enlargement is necessarily reflected in institutional consensus about how best to secure those interests. Grand statements on the overarching importance of enlargement for Germany have persistently been flanked by departmental, territorial and/or sectional interests pursuing their own narrower concerns. In this sense, enlargement politics, like the 1996–97 IGC, is more characteristic of German EU diplomacy than EMU: while the longer-term strategic goal may be quite clear, its realisation can be clouded by the tactical confusion of short-term institutional parochialism. This was certainly the case under the leadership of Helmut Kohl; little has changed under his successor, Gerhard Schröder.

Domestic policy formulation for enlargement

Like the IGC policy process, enlargement policy-making in Germany has in principle been highly inclusive, reflecting the fact that almost all federal ministries' remits (and the sectional interests of many of their client groups) are touched in one way or another by the implications of enlargement. Equally, at least half of the Länder (and their respective client interests) are directly engaged in addressing the current or future implications of opening up to the East. However, the occasions on which this institutional pluralism has been let loose in enlargement policymaking were, until the debate on the Commission's Agenda 2000 proposals of 1997, rare.

For much of the period before 1997, enlargement was in the main a concern of EU 'high politics' and detached from the everyday cut and thrust of domestic institutional interaction. This gave the triumvirate of lead EU policy departments – the Foreign Office, the Economics Ministry and, periodically, the Chancellor's Office[5] – the leeway to make progress on the overarching German interest in stabilisation/security. In these circumstances, a number of EU-level deals could be cut which allowed Germany to maintain an (at times precarious) balance between widening and deepening, and between old commitments to France and new commitments to the East: the cautious opening gambit of setting up the Europe Agreements while simultaneously digesting the jump forward in deepening launched at Maastricht; the brokering of the deal during the 1994 German EU Presidency which concretised a pre-accession strategy for the associated states while also throwing the French the bone of a beefed-up Mediterranean policy to gnaw on; and the careful maintenance of enlargement at a reasonable heat on the back boiler of EU decision-making, while attention was necessarily focused elsewhere on the IGC and the run-up to the launch of EMU.[6]

The negotiation of the Europe Agreements in 1991 had, however, revealed a rather different pattern of policy-making redolent of earlier episodes of sectorisation, with 'the German stance ... badly coordinated at best, contradictory at worst'.[7] Since this is a pattern of policy-making which has returned to the fore since 1997, it is worth dwelling on for a moment. The most important features of the Europe Agreements were the steps taken to remove barriers to trade between the EU and the associated states. The agreed principle was that this should occur asymmetrically to the benefit of the CEE countries; in other words, EU markets would be opened up to them at a quicker pace than their markets to the EU. Predictably, the asymmetry principle foundered on the rock of national producer interests within the EU, notably in agriculture, textiles and steel. While much of this protectionist impulse came from elsewhere in the EU, it resided in part in attempts by some German ministries to protect their clients' markets. It is hardly surprising that the Ministry of Agriculture and a fairly uncompetitive farming sector figured strongly here; more surprising was the protectionist stance of an Economics Ministry which had developed a notable free-trade pedigree throughout the postwar era.[8] The inconsistency with the stabilisation/security strategy which set the general guideline for German policy is clear:

> Although Germany as a whole has the strongest interest among EU members in stability in CEE, concessions to some sectors of domestic industry led to a highly restrictive stance on market access in the EA [European Agreement] negotiations. Not only does this contradict a strictly economic logic, if one takes into account the considerable future export opportunities for German industry, but in the broader political context it undermined an otherwise consistent political strategy which combined substantial financial aid with support for eventual membership.[9]

The Europe Agreements thus revealed a split between ministries committed to overarching goals – the Foreign Office and the Chancellor's Office – and others rooted more directly in domestic interests. This was a constellation which re-emerged six years later when enlargement again descended from the reaches of high politics to impinge on baser – and harder – economic interests. The catalyst here was Agenda 2000, which concretised the fact that eastern enlargement would require existing member states to sacrifice some current benefits and/or contribute more to the EU's costs. Most controversial were those aspects of the Agenda focused on what to do with high-cost common policies – CAP and the Structural Funds – which, if left unreformed, would be unfinancable if applied in an enlarged EU; and how to reshape the EU's financial framework to meet the challenges the run-up to enlargement would pose. Agenda 2000, in other words, touched on matters of tangible material interest in the member states: farming subsidies, structural funding allocations and levels of contribution to the EU budget. Correctly, Chancellor Kohl expected 'massive punch-ups on the matter'[10] between the member states; he perhaps did not expect there to be so many 'punch-ups on the matter' within Germany or within his own government.

A vital factor in the Agenda 2000 debate was the prominent role assumed by the Finance Ministry on the question of EU budget reform, or what domestically became known as the *Nettozahlerdebatte*, the 'net contributor debate'. The Finance Ministry's concern to limit the German contribution to the EU budget was not a new one, figuring strongly for example in the budget debates launched by Mrs Thatcher's handbag in the early 1980s.[11] What had changed was the context: by the mid-1990s Germany's net contributions made up around 60 per cent of the EU total. This figure looked even more striking against a domestic economic backdrop of post-unity fiscal rigour, reinforced by the dash to meet the criteria for EMU, and high unemployment. What had also changed was the authority and vigour with which the Finance Ministry sought concessions on the issue in the late 1990s. This reflected in a general sense the increased Euro-political role and experience the Finance Ministry had taken on in the EMU era. It also reflected, and drew quite explicitly on, *popular* fears that the costs of the forthcoming enlargement, like all its predecessors, would be borne by a German taxpayer already 'suffering' for (EMU-)Europe.[12] As in the case of EMU on the issue of currency stability, clear public support legitimised and strengthened a tough policy line.

An additional dose of toughness came out of Bavaria, where the CSU Minister-President Edmund Stoiber was pressing for a tough line on the Commission's budget proposals in Agenda 2000 'reminiscent of Thatcher's pugnacity over the British rebate during the 1980s'.[13] Stoiber's pugnacity undoubtedly had an impact on his rival for pre-eminence in the CSU, Finance Minister Waigel, stiffening his resolve that 'eastern enlargement should not cost one pfennig more to the German tax payer'.[14] The net effect was – surprisingly – to move Helmut Kohl over the last twelve months of his Chancellorship to pursue a specifically national concern – the 'correction of budgetary imbalances'[15] – ahead of his more characteristic, strategic view of EU matters in general and eastern enlargement more specifically.

The pursuit of national concerns was mirrored in the CAP reform debate provoked by Agenda 2000. Significant reform to the CAP, which still consumes half the EU budget, is without doubt *the* vital financial precondition for enlargement. However, German agriculture has typically been both inefficient in world market terms and – at least as long as a Christian Democrat was in charge of the Agriculture Ministry – a massively influential domestic lobby. The latter reflects the electoral importance of the farming vote to the CDU/CSU and presents the only point on which there has been a clear party-political difference in enlargement policy. While generally a broad party-political consensus on enlargement-related matters has prevailed, agriculture divides the CDU/CSU from the SPD, whose lack of sympathy for agricultural concerns was reflected in a stronger willingness to contemplate reform of the CAP after the change of government in September 1998. However, until that point, agricultural policy was a classically 'captured' field in which significant reform – even that suggested by other Federal Government departments![16] – was inconceivable.

The net result was an extraordinarily contradictory stance which, to the annoyance of Germany's EU partners,[17] proposed the unrealistic combination of advocating enlargement as a top priority; stressing the need, though, to reduce the German contribution to the EU budget; while blocking progress in the search for reform of CAP, without which meaningful reform of the structure of the EU budget was scarcely possible. This logically untenable position was the legacy bequeathed to the SPD–Green government elected in September 1998. It was also a legacy which had to be mastered quickly, given that Germany took over the Presidency of the EU on 1 January 1999 and that the deadline for a deal on Agenda 2000 had been set for March 1999.

In some key respects, the change of government set new parameters for addressing Agenda 2000/enlargement policy. Most fundamental was generational change. As Timothy Garton-Ash put it, pondering life after Kohl in 1994: 'It is far from certain that the Euro-idealism of the middle and younger generations in Germany is as widespread or deep as that of the immediate postwar generation.'[18] Gerhard Schröder confirmed this shortly after assuming power:

> My generation and those following *are Europeans because we want to be not because we have to be. That makes us freer in dealing with others* ... I am convinced that our European partners want to have a self-confident German partner which is more calculable than a German partner with an inferiority complex. *Germany standing up for its national interests will be just as natural as France or Britain standing up for theirs.*[19]

Schröder's intention to 'stand up for' national interests spawned a rather more forthright tone of EU policy debate than had been typical under Kohl. The central issue remained, though, Germany's status as the biggest net payer into the EU budget, or, as Schröder put it, the problem that 'the Germans pay more than half the contributions which are *frittered away* [*verbraten*] in Europe'.[20] Such vigorous language of national interest versus Euro-profligacy set the scene for the new government's contribution to the ongoing Agenda 2000 debate. This new tone was also flanked by two other changes. First, the EU policy coordination responsibilities of the Economics Ministry were transferred to the Finance Ministry (see Chapter 2). This cemented the upgrading of the Finance Ministry's status which had arisen with EMU and – again reinforced by a cost-conscious public opinion – bolstered the tough line on the EU budget taken by Schröder.[21] Second, agriculture lost its privileged status and immunity to reform under a government led by the 'workers" party.

The changed parameters under Schröder allowed a more plausible policy position to emerge. First, at the launch of the Presidency it was reaffirmed that: 'We neither can nor will solve Europe's problems with a German cheque-book.'[22] In other words, as enlargement approached, others would have to forego privileges to relieve the pressure on the German net contribution: Britain its rebate, Spain the Cohesion Fund and, most significantly, France a part of its benefits from the CAP. The latter intimation pointed to the second component of the Schröder position: a new openness to CAP reform, in particular the move towards an element of national co-financing of farming support.

Though this position may have been more plausible and coherent than that of Kohl, it was still neither uncontroversial nor more acceptable. Both in Germany and beyond, Schröder's more overtly 'national' position was for some unsettling.[23] More generally, as it was Germany's responsibility to pilot Agenda 2000 to a conclusion during the EU Presidency, an honest-broker position would have been more appropriate than making such tough demands of its partners. The need to assume the brokering role was, however, brought home when the European Commission resigned on 15 March 1999, undermining the support and implementation capacities available to the Presidency. The outbreak of hostilities in Kosovo nine days later also dragged attention elsewhere. In these circumstances, the important question rapidly became less one of resolving German budgetary concerns than of whether any kind of agreement could be reached on Agenda 2000 by the Berlin Summit scheduled for the end of the month.[24]

The solution which emerged in these conditions was not one which matched up too well against Schröder's earlier rhetoric. There was no substantial reform of the CAP, and certainly no new national co-financing arrangement, which was ritually blocked by France. And the outcome only tinkered at the margins of the Cohesion Fund, the British rebate and the size of the German net contribution (cut only by roughly 300 million Euro yearly). Nevertheless, Agenda 2000, with its crucial financial framework for 2000–06 was packed off into its implementation phase, meeting a crucial precondition for the enlargement process.[25] In other words, faced with the reality of EU policy-making and the responsibilities of the Presidency, Schröder compromised his specifically national aims and brokered (and in effect continued to fund) an EU-wide deal.

This triumph of Euro-pragmatism might seem at first sight an outcome of 'after Kohl, *plus ça change!*'. However, if one looks beyond the disciplines imposed by the Presidency and more closely at Schröder's original conception of the Agenda 2000 issue, one can discern the outline of a change in approach. It is less easy to see with Schröder the underlying importance of the stabilisation/security nexus which drove on enlargement policy under Kohl. This may in part be because progress on enlargement has already stabilised and secured Germany's immediate east sufficiently. There is also a sense, though, that Schröder's approach – as reinforced by the formal upgrading of the Finance Ministry in EU matters – is to make more open and 'rational' calculations of cost and benefit in EU policy, and to define policy choices in this way. This might be called a 'yes, but ...' politics in the context of enlargement: a basic commitment to implementing enlargement, but hedged with conditions to soften its implications for Germany. During his first EU Summit in Austrian Pörtschach in October 1998 Schröder stressed, for example, that the EU should not raise false expectations in the accession countries, because enlargement was a much more difficult and long-term process than had been anticipated, for which, 'realistically, we will need time'.[26] It was also notable how Schröder pushed very strongly for Gunter Verheugen, his nominee as European Commissioner in the renewal of the Commission in 1999, to be awarded the eastern enlargement portfolio. This broke the mould in German personnel policy on the Commission two ways. First, Verheugen is a candidate of stature, unlike many of his predecessors. And second, it pitched a German nominee quite explicitly into a field of particular national concern.

The change of tone under Schröder and the Verheugen appointment have both confirmed the new 'yes, but ...' approach. This approach is becoming increasingly evident as the accession negotiations begun in March 1998 move through the agenda to reach the more contentious chapters on matters such as the Single Market – the free movement of labour in particular – and internal security. German policy-makers are unlikely to budge easily from their concerns to win long transition periods to insulate German labour markets, especially in low-skill sectors, from cheaper migrant labour from the east, or to insist on tougher border controls in the accession states as the EU's external border shifts eastwards. The accession states' negotiators should not expect an easy ride.

This is all the more so since the Länder are now deeply involved through their nominated representatives in the accession negotiations. During the 1990s, the Länder have gone through a conversion from an unreservedly positive and unanimous stance on the principle and desirability of enlargement to one also hedged by a range of 'yes, but ...' qualifications.[27] A classic example was the quite overtly protectionist response to the competitive challenge of enlargement by the Saxon government in 1996, when it (illegally) awarded a DM 779 million subsidy to secure a Volkswagen investment. Saxony's argument – lost in a legal battle with the Commission – was that if the subsidy were not allowed, then Volkswagen would transfer its investment further east, where labour costs were cheaper.[28] This attempt to protect jobs against the low (labour) cost competition which the enlargement process is increasingly generating is certainly not an isolated example; eastern Germany is arguably the most heavily subsidised region of the EU, and additional attempts to prevent the 'export' of jobs eastwards can surely be expected in the coming years. This essentially protectionist impulse was also revealed in a different context in the sustained, and ultimately highly successful campaign by the eastern Länder to ward off the threat the Agenda 2000 discussions posed to their highest priority, Objective One status under the Funds.[29] If enlargement required cost-cutting – as all agreed – then it had to be someone else's costs which had to be cut.

Unsurprisingly, Bavaria has also been prominent in enlargement-related debates. This prominence has two sources. First, Bavaria has exploited the opportunity enlargement presents for 'issue linkage',[30] for using issues raised by enlargement as a means indirectly of furthering other political agendas. Policy papers published on the CAP in 1995 and the Structural Funds in 1996 were prominent examples; though published in the context of what would become the Agenda 2000 debates, they had little to do with preparing for enlargement as such, and rather more with using the implications of enlargement as a pretext for

Eastern enlargement 113

pushing forward Bavarian agendas on subsidiarity and deregulation.[31] Second, Bavaria is an eastern Land, located on the enlargement borderline and just as exercised by the concrete implications of enlargement as the new Länder further north or federal ministries working on extending the Single Market or internal security policy eastwards. In fact some of the tougher and more restrictive proposals on these issues have come from Bavaria.[32]

What insights do these observations open up on German policy in the accession negotiations? Barbara Lippert rather chillingly described the opening of these negotiations in March 1998 as a shift 'into the phase of bureaucratic politics' characterised 'by the governments of the member states defending [their] possessions'.[33] This comment suggests Germany is not alone in pursuing narrow national interests in the context of enlargement (although, as a result of the change of government in 1998, it may do so in a rather more hard-nosed, cost-focused way than its partners have hitherto been accustomed to). Where Germany does clearly differ is in the nature of the fragmented, highly sectorised government structures which are pursuing those interests. This is all the more so, since the enlargement negotiations have reached a stage in which the issues have become technical and detailed, and are less subject to purposeful coordination than they were in the earlier period of high politics under the Kohl governments.

This should not lead inevitably (just) to a negative conclusion about institutional pluralism gone wild. While the involved federal ministries and Länder will undoubtedly work hard to defend their particular institutional 'possessions' in the accession negotiations, none of them is ever going to question the desirability of enlargement in principle, and most of them have taken active steps to facilitate enlargement. On this other, facilitative side of the balance sheet there has developed a mass of activities led by German policy actors which – albeit highly sectorised and profoundly uncoordinated – are doing much to put the groundwork of an enlarged EU in place. The German Interior Ministry has supported the modernisation of the Polish and Czech border policing infrastructure. Growing economic interaction with the German public and private sector seems to be establishing German-style patterns of regulation in the CEE economies.[34] Cross-border cooperation between the eastern Länder and their counterparts across the Polish and Czech borders is removing barriers to integration and generating grass roots 'social capital' to flesh out the formal integration process.[35] There are countless know-how and personnel exchanges under way at all levels,[36] with the political foundations playing, as in previous enlargement rounds, a major role.

The net effect of all this is incalculable, but highly significant. In an entirely uncoordinated way, disconnected from the hard-ball politics of the enlargement negotiations, myriad aspects of Germany's institutional and regulatory structures are being 'exported' into CEE. This 'export' process recalls the earlier comment about enlargement as milieu goal. It is, however, a rather different form of milieu shaping than that discussed earlier in Chapter 1 of this book, which involved the virtuous circle arising from indirect institutional power deployed as a result of the German instinct to seek multilateral solutions and the consequent process of 'systemic empowerment' by the multilateral structures thus created. In the enlargement context, institutional export is 'pre-emptively' diffusing German norms in CEE *outside of* the EU's current multilateral framework; the milieu is thus being shaped without the involvement of Germany's existing partners in multilateral cooperation and stands to 'pay back' asymmetrically in Germany's favour once enlargement is realised. The effect is potentially of tremendous significance for German power and systemic empowerment in the post-enlargement EU. This potential was expressed with unusual candour by Christoph Jessen, head of the German Foreign Office Department responsible for the Agenda 2000 negotiations:

> Germany ... profits ... from the extension of the familiar milieu [*vertrauten Raumes*] in which common norms, *most of which have been decisively shaped by Germany*, come to be applied. Any adaptation costs arising from this fall to member states which are less strongly able to shape these norms. *In this way benefits accrue to Germany which are numerically scarcely verifiable but nevertheless considerable.*[37]

The informal but pervasive milieu shaping arising from institutional export can, as Jessen states, only benefit Germany, while holding implicit disadvantage for others. It is to the 'others' the discussion now turns in an exploration of how the depth and implications of German interests and involvement in the enlargement process have impacted on relations with France, the Netherlands and the UK.

Relations with partners

France

These comments on milieu shaping have a particular resonance in the French case. It has been a persistent theme in this book that the

Franco–German relationship which has driven European integration on has undergone a notable balance of adjustment since 1990 in Germany's favour. Nowhere has this been more overt than in the question of enlargement. In at least three respects, the enlargement process has disturbed the old Franco–German equilibrium:[38]

- First, the prospect of eastern enlargement confirmed that Germany's freedom of manoeuvre in European politics stood to be increased by the post-1989 changes, with its postwar *Einbindung* in a Francocentric Western Europe correspondingly loosened.
- Second, had the Cold War not ended, developing the EU's outreach around and across the Mediterranean would have been a top priority project – and, of course, one in which France had and has a deep security interest; the imperative of dealing with the EU's eastward relations after the end of the Cold War has pushed European *Südpolitik* – and French security – way down the agenda.
- Third, geographical proximity and the rapid regeneration of intensive economic interaction across the old Cold War borders rapidly established Germany as the most influential player in CEE (a position since further reinforced by the institutional milieu shaping noted (see above), and have shifted the EU's centre of gravity towards the German north-east and away from France.[39]

The French response has typically been to try to act as a brake on the enlargement process. President Mitterrand's 1990 notion of a confederal structure for Europe was an initial example. While denying the CEE countries direct membership of the EU, this would still have offered CEE a framework for cooperation, but one loose enough not 'to interfere with the process of tying Germany down in the west'.[40] Mitterrand's comment in this context that CEE states would have to wait 'for decades' for membership was, however, rapidly overtaken by events[41] as Germany's (and a wider European) stabilisation/security imperative culminated in the 1991 Europe Agreements.

An alternative, more realistic and certainly more enduring strategy was to make the implementation of the enlargement process launched by the Europe Agreements contingent on deepening. This was a formula which offered the prospect of an irrevocable *Einbindung* of Germany before enlargement loosened its ties to the (French-led) West and/or weakened the cohesion of the EU by diluting it into little more than a free trade area. It was clearly reflected in the EMU project and timetable agreed at Maastricht, with the DM to be subsumed into EMU by the end of the century and certainly before even the most optimistic dates for enlargement. It did not, though, solve the problem entirely, as Germany continued to oscillate between its roles as deepener and widener of integration. Nevertheless – or because of this – the theme of deepening before widening remained a persistent feature of French European diplomacy through to the 1996–97 IGC and beyond. The IGC was, of course, supposed to come up with proposals for institutional deepening which would allow an enlarged EU to function. Given that it largely failed to do so, it was characteristic that France (together with Belgium and Italy) was signatory to a declaration appended to the Amsterdam Treaty stating that the Treaty 'does not meet the need ... for substantial progress towards strengthening of the institutions' and that 'such strengthening is a prerequisite to the conclusion of the first accession negotiations'.[42] The theme reappeared, against the background of the accession negotiations begun in March 1998, in the French insistence on a 'controlled enlargement' in which the 'Leitmotif'[43] of institutional reform as precondition for enlargement has repeatedly been restated.[44]

The task of securing a fundamental German interest in enlargement alongside a long-standing one in deepening, nuanced by the need to keep its traditional partner on board, has been a major challenge for German policy-makers through the 1990s. Solutions have varied. Probably least successful was the 'hard core' idea proposed by Schäuble–Lamers (see Chapter 2). This offered a clever combination of deepening and widening, with a Franco–German 'core of the hard core' proceeding ahead to EMU amid patterns of differentiated integration extending out from the core – with variations across policy areas – to include existing and future (i.e. CEE) member states. The tenor of the paper was though one which was deeply sceptical about the possibility and desirability of Italian and other south European membership in EMU. The paper was regarded with deep suspicion in France. As Patrick McCarthy put it: 'To be locked up in a box with Germany and the Netherlands was to risk having no influence over the future European Central Bank and falling under German domination.'[45] The hard core idea consequently fizzled out, reappearing only in mildest form in the provisions for 'flexibility' arising from the 1996–97 IGC.

More effective was the Weimar Triangle, which grew out of a meeting of the German, French and Polish Foreign Ministers in August 1991 into an institutionalised arrangement, also involving in due course the respective Defence Ministers and heads of government. The Triangle rested on a complex balance of national interests.[46] For Poland it was a vehicle which offered the prospect of smoothing its accession to the EU, while also moderating Germany's influence in the region via French input. For France it offered access to and, possibly, influence over German enlargement policy, as Christian Deubner put it, 'a place at Germany's side' in the east.[47] For Germany, it was a vehicle for opening out the stabilisation process it had hitherto largely funded in CEE and placing it in a multilateral framework. More generally, it helped to routinise enlargement policy in Franco–German discussions, co-opting France at least in part into the role of integration widener. This provided a foundation for subsequent initiatives to be flown under the heading of Franco–German leadership, in particular during the consecutive French and German Presidencies in 1994.

There was a gear change in enlargement policy in 1994. This was partly fuelled by the formal membership applications tabled by Hungary and Poland in the Spring. Further impetus was added by the growing German desire, in the light of a difficult domestic economic situation, to multilateralise (the funding of) CEE stabilisation policy. This desire was consummated through the Franco–German tandem which, in a series of joint declarations and bilateral meetings, pre-decided the pre-accession strategy adopted at the Essen Summit in December. The quid pro quo was German agreement – at significant extra cost to the EU budget – to develop a stronger Mediterranean policy capable of addressing stabilisation issues raised by the Algerian civil war.[48]

The Weimar Triangle and a beefed-up Mediterranean policy together offered a partial rebalancing of the Franco–German relationship in France's interests, with the French able now to look over Germany's shoulders into the East on the one hand, and to claim a revival of the EU's Mediterranean presence on the other. There have, however, been no equivalent triumphs for France since then. There is no sense that the braking tactic of deepening before widening has had any effect as the accession negotiations have taken shape. More than that, though, the change of government in Germany in 1998, with its tougher emphasis on costs and benefits, has suggested that no more side-payments, such as Mediterranean policy, will be forthcoming. It was striking also how, in the Agenda 2000 negotiations, the Schröder government was unabashed in attacking French CAP privileges with an openness scarcely conceivable under Helmut Kohl. Though Schröder backed down under the pressures of the 1999 Presidency, Germany's 'new realism'[49] does not augur well for Franco–German concord, as each seeks to defend its 'possessions' as the accession negotiations and related adjustments to existing EU policy provision pan out.

The Netherlands

For Koen Koch, the Netherlands did not have much of an enlargement policy through to the mid-1990s.[50] Encouraged by its maritime tradition, the Netherlands stood steadfastly with 'its back to the continent' throughout the Cold War. Only in 1992 was a policy paper produced which sought to come to terms with the implications for the Netherlands of the end of the Cold War and its concomitant, EU enlargement. Even this was hardly enthusiastic, echoing the French position that enlargement, though necessary, had to be preceded by deepening, and should not affect the 'quality of the Community' as reflected in the *acquis communautaire*. There was also an echo of the French fear that enlargement implicitly loosened German *Einbindung*, and therefore that a deepening process which would bind Germany in more tightly to its (Western) partners was necessary:

> The government believes that the accession of further new members should be preceded by a fundamental reform of the way in which EU institutions operate, with a view to both the efficiency and decisiveness of the Union in its various policy fields *and the active participation of Germany in the process of European integration*.[51]

In other words, enlargement has been perceived very much as a threat to a comfortable status quo, and Dutch policy has been to ward off as much of this threat as possible. The perception of enlargement-as-threat has reappeared elsewhere in the context of the likely downgrading of the representation of small states in EU institutions in the course of pre-enlargement institutional reform,[52] and of the financial implications of enlargement to the Netherlands, already a moderate net contributor.[53]

These are hardly positions which create a strong basis for cooperation with Germany, not least because they still reflect, despite the wider improvement of Dutch–German relations since the early 1990s, historical suspicions which require Germany to be bound in to EU-Europe. There have certainly been no notable meetings of minds or joint initiatives in the various stages of the enlargement process hitherto. However, Agenda 2000 did reveal a commonality which may open up ground for cooperation in the accession negotiations and in EU policy reform; a commitment to achieving enlargement 'at acceptable costs'. Described by Koch as a 'return of the national interest', this aspiration – and its focal points in EU budget restructuring and 'thorough revision' of the CAP – chime very much with that of the new Schröder government.[54] If one takes into account commonalities with the UK position too, a coalition for serious pre-enlargement reform begins to emerge.

The UK

Perhaps rather oddly, the UK is the EU member state whose population is unusually well-disposed to enlargement, and whose governments have been consistent supporters of a rapid and comprehensive enlargement process. However, the former point reflects the fact that 'clearly, few British people know where these countries are',[55] and the latter has reflected ulterior motive. Since 1989, enlargement has been favoured by British governments as an instrument to secure other interests, notably to make substantial deepening impossible. This position was put forward most nakedly by Margaret Thatcher. As *The Times* elegantly put it: 'Eastern Europe is Mrs Thatcher's Trojan horse. Wheeled into the corridors of Brussels, it will disgorge a thousand threats to the oligopolies of the EC.'[56] Successor governments under John Major and Tony Blair have also sought to instrumentalise enlargement for other ends, Major in a softer version of Thatcher's anti-deepening tactic, Blair to secure reform elsewhere, notably to the CAP.

This is not an especially promising basis for developing UK–German alliances. There has consistently been a lack of serious engagement in the UK with a topic which 'does not bulk as large on the British horizon as it does for some other EC members',[57] Germany in particular. And Germany has sought to reconcile deepening and widening rather than to play on their apparent incompatibilities (as France and the Netherlands have also done, but in the opposite context of deepening to delay widening). Nonetheless, a basis for UK–German cooperation on the issue has begun to emerge as the concrete details and implications of enlargement come to be negotiated. Most obvious is a coalition of interest on policy and budgetary reform prior to enlargement. In particular 'reform of the CAP' is felt to be 'long overdue' by the Blair government and if addressed would provide a way of dealing with the iniquities of the EU budget: 'The best way of keeping member states' contributions to affordable levels is to ensure firm control of the Union's spending. We hope that Germany will join us in pressing for fundamental reform of the CAP, which will bring savings in the longer term.'[58]

This invitation was not taken up in the Agenda 2000 negotiations but, given the obvious coalition of interests and the new spirit of cooperation between Blair and Schröder, it could be in future. More generally, the outline of a northern coalition on pre-enlargement reform also including the Netherlands and perhaps the Scandinavian states, tendentially ranged against CAP-supporting France and the net-recipient south, becomes visible. This is not to suggest that an enduring north–south divide will come into play, but rather that the concrete implications raised for the existing EU as enlargement nears have produced keener conceptions of national interests and 'possessions'. It is the interaction of these – rather than a Franco–German relationship still trying to make the 'momentous adjustment'[59] to the post-1989 era – which seems set to drive the final phases of enlargement decision-making through to the point of accession.

Notes

1. M. Singer and A. Wildavsky, *The Real World Order. Zones of Peace, Zones of Turmoil* (Chatham: Chatham House Publishers, 1996).
2. Ultimately, separate agreements with the divided Czech and Slovak Republics were signed; further agreements were concluded with Bulgaria and Romania in 1993.
3. M. Jopp, 'Germany and EU Enlargement', in K. Kaiser and M. Brüning (eds), *East-Central Europe and the EU: Problems of Integration* (Bonn: Europa Union Verlag, 1996), 107.
4. Cf. H. Tewes, 'Between Deepening and Widening: Role Conflict in Germany's Enlargement Policy', *West European Politics*, 21 (1998).
5. With each taking the lead at different points. The Economics Ministry was most prominent in and around the negotiation of the Europe Agreements, the Foreign Office thereafter, and in particular with the creation of its Enlargement Working Team in 1994. Reflecting Helmut Kohl's policy interests, the Chancellor's Office was also heavily engaged in ensuring Kohl's *Richtlinienkompetenz* was observed. For a full account of inter-ministerial division of labour and policy coordination in the field, see S. Collins, 'Managing the Agenda? German Policy-Making with Regard to Eastern Enlargement of the European Union', Ph.D. dissertation, Institute for German Studies, University of Birmingham, 1999.
6. The best account of the ways in which German policy-makers managed their at times acute role conflicts as integration deepeners and integration wideners is in H. Tewes, 'Germany as a Civilian Power. The Western Integration of East Central Europe', Ph.D. dissertation, Institute for German Studies, University of Birmingham, 1999.
7. Ibid., 142.
8. Ibid.
9. U. Sedelmeier, 'The European Union's Association Policy Towards Central and Eastern Europe', *Sussex European Institute Discussion Paper* (1994), 14.
10. As reported in *Frankfurter Allgemeine Zeitung*, 22 April 1998, and quoted in J. Janning, 'Bundesrepublik Deutschland', in W. Weidenfeld and W. Wessels (eds), *Jahrbuch der Europäischen Integration 1997/98* (Bonn: Europa Union Verlag, 1999), 315.

11 Bulmer and Paterson, *The Federal Republic of Germany and the European Community*, 67–71.
12 Institut für Europäische Politik (ed.), *Enlargement/Agenda 2000 Watch*, Pilot Issue (October 1998), 19.
13 N. Proudfoot, 'Europeanisation and the New Regionalism. The Case of Bavaria', M.Phil. dissertation, University of Cambridge, 1997, 67.
14 Quoted in Tewes, 'Between Deepening and Widening', 129.
15 Cf. B. Lippert, 'Die Erweiterungspolitik der Europäischen Union', in Weidenfeld and Wessels (eds), *Jahrbuch der Europäischen Integration 1997/98*, 44. See also 'Gipfeltreffen der Staats- und Regierungschefs in Cardiff. Kohl will deutschen EU-Beitrag senken', *Süddeutsche Zeitung* 16 June 1998.
16 I.e. a Finance Ministry concerned for obvious reasons to break the log-jam of CAP reform, in this case by proposing a national co-financing arrangement for farming support. Cf. Institut für Europäische Politik (ed.), *Enlargement/Agenda 2000 Watch*, Pilot Issue (October 1998), 52.
17 Cf. B. Lippert, 'Der Gipfel von Luxemburg: Startschuß für das Abenteuer Erweiterung', *Integration*, 21 (1998), 22–3.
18 T. Garton-Ash, 'Germany's Choice', *Foreign Affairs*, 73 (1994), 74.
19 Quoted in 'Germany – Annual Country Review', *Financial Times*, 10 November 1998, 6. Our italics.
20 Our italics. *'Verbraten'* in the original. Quoted in G. Langguth, 'Ein sozialistisches Europa? Ist die These "vom Ende des sozialdemokratischen Jahrhunderts" widerlegt?', *Politische Studien*, 50 (1999), 55.
21 Interviews with Finance Ministry representatives in June 1999 suggested the switch from Economics to Finance has resulted in the emergence of a more 'streamlined', 'efficient' and 'realistic' approach to EU policy matters.
22 Schröder, quoted in the *Guardian*, 2 January 1999.
23 F. Pflüger, 'Europa muß Weltmacht werden. Weichenstellungen der deutschen Ratspräsidentschaft', *Internationale Politik* (1999), 58; *Independent*, 13 December 1998.
24 *Die Welt*, 27 February 1999.
25 *Handelsblatt*, 29 March 1999.
26 Quoted in 'Germany – Annual Country Review', *Financial Times*, 10 November 1998, 6. See also *EU-Magazin*, December, 1998, 19.
27 Cf. Jeffery, 'The German Länder and the "Normalisation" of the EU Enlargement Debate'.
28 As documented in the collection *Teilungsfolgen. Materialsammlung zum Streit um staatliche Beihilfe an die Volkswagen AG für ein Investitionsvorhaben im Freistaat Sachsen* (Dresden: Sächsische Staatskanzlei, 1996).
29 C. Jeffery and S. Collins, 'The German Länder and EU Enlargement: Between Apple Pie and Issue Linkage', *German Politics*, 7 (1998), 97–8.
30 Ibid.
31 Cf. Jeffery, 'The German Länder and the "Normalisation" of the EU Enlargement Debate'.

32 E.g. a proposal by the CSU for a transition period on free movement of labour extending to 2015 (Institut für Europäische Politik (ed.), *Enlargement/Agenda 2000 Watch*, Pilot Issue (October 1998), 27), or the suggestion by the Bavarian Ministry of the Interior that applicant states be required to provide effective (i.e. Bavarian-standard) levels of security at their external borders 'before accession' (*Europa aktuell. Ein Info-Service der Bayerischen Staatskanzlei*, December 1998).
33 Lippert, 'Die Erweiterungspolitik der Europäischen Union', 38.
34 Cf. P. Katzenstein, 'Germany and Mitteleuropa', in P. Katzenstein (ed.), *Mitteleuropa. Between Europe and Germany* (Oxford: Berghahn, 1997).
35 Jeffery and Collins, 'The German Länder and EU Enlargement', 99–100.
36 The Land of Berlin alone can claim some 240 agencies involved in advice, consultancy, education and training in the CEE states. *Zusammenarbeit des Landes Berlin mit Mittel- und Osteuropa*, Senatskanzlei E 11, Bonn, 13 January 1999.
37 C. Jessen, 'Agenda 2000: Das Reformpaket von Berlin, ein Erfolg für Gesamteuropa', *Integration*, 22 (1999), 168. Our italics.
38 H. Unterwedde, 'Deutsch-Französische Beziehungen: Perspektiven einer spannungsgeladenen Partnerschaft', *Politische Studien*, 49 (1998), 13. The following points are drawn from C. Deubner, 'Frankreich in der Osterweiterung der EU, 1989 bis 1997', *Politische Studien*, 50 (1999), 93–5.
39 The EFTAn enlargement of 1995 had a similar effect, compounding French concerns.
40 P. McCarthy, 'France, Germany, the IGC and Eastern Enlargement', in D. Webber (ed.), *The Franco–German Relationship in the European Union* (London: Routledge, 1999), 44.
41 Notably the breakdown of the former Soviet Union in 1991 and the first stirrings of the wars of Yugoslav succession in 1992.
42 Quoted in Institut für Europäische Politik (ed.), *Enlargement/Agenda 2000 Watch*, 43.
43 F. de la Serre and C. Lequesne, 'Frankreich', in Weidenfeld and Wessels (eds), *Jahrbuch der Europäischen Integration 1997/98*, 335.
44 Cf. ibid.; Institut für Europäische Politik (ed.), *Enlargement/Agenda 2000 Watch*, 23, 43–4; Lippert, 'Der Gipfel von Luxemburg', 24–5.
45 McCarthy, 'France, Germany, the IGC and Eastern Enlargement', 49.
46 The following draws on Tewes, 'Germany as a Civilian Power. The Western Integration of East Central Europe'.
47 Deubner, 'Frankreich in der Osterweiterung der EU', 104.
48 de la Serre and Lequesne, 'Frankreich', 312–13.
49 C. Jeffery and V. Handl, 'Germany and Europe after Kohl: Between Social Democracy and Normalisation?', *Birmingham One Europe Discussion Papers* (2000).
50 K. Koch, 'The Netherlands and EU Enlargement', in K. Kaiser and M. Brüning (eds), *East-Central Europe and the EU: Problems of Integration* (Bonn: Europa Union Verlag, 1996), 121–4.

51 Quoted in ibid., 133. Our italics.
52 M. Kwast-van Duursen, 'Niederlande', in W. Weidenfeld and W. Wessels (eds), *Jahrbuch der Europäischen Integration 1995/96* (Bonn: Europa Union Verlag, 1997), 335.
53 A. Pijpers and J. Rood, 'Niederlande', in Weidenfeld and Wessels (eds), *Jahrbuch der Europäischen Integration 1997/98*, 358–60.
54 K. Koch, 'The Netherlands and EU Enlargement', in K. Kaiser and M. Brüning (eds), *East-Central Europe and the EU: Problems of Integration* (Bonn: Europa Union Verlag, 1996), 141–2.
55 Institut für Europäische Politik (ed.), *Enlargement/Agenda 2000 Watch*, 22.
56 *The Times*, 6 August 1990, quoted in H. Tewes, 'Germany as a Civilian Power. The Western Integration of East Central Europe'.
57 J. Hayward, 'Britain and EU Enlargement', in K. Kaiser and M. Brüning (eds), *East-Central Europe and the EU: Problems of Integration* (Bonn: Europa Union Verlag, 1996), 148.
58 Former Agriculture Minister Jack Cunningham in July 1998. Quoted in Institut für Europäische Politik (ed.), *Enlargement/Agenda 2000 Watch*, 55–6.
59 Deubner, 'Frankreich in der Osterweiterung der EU', 93.

7

Conclusions

The domestic and European arenas of German European diplomacy

It was suggested in our introduction that a narrow interest-driven focus to the study of German European diplomacy, such as that favoured in realist analyses of international politics, is inadequate. Germany is manifestly not a realist state, pursuing its interests on specific issues on a case-by-case basis and acting accordingly, as the realist paradigm would demand. Rather, Germany has pursued, in a more strategic sense, broad-based and diffuse milieu goals, directed at shaping wider conditions of inter-state interaction and, above all, *cooperation* beyond national boundaries. As we have argued, an understanding of this milieu-shaping approach requires a fuller consideration of the institutional and identitive dimensions of Germany's European diplomacy than narrow realist approaches would or could concede.

A realist approach would assume (at the risk of over-simplification) that 'the state' is a monolithic foreign-policy actor, engaged in a form of zero-sum competition with the other states in the international system to secure some 'national interest' derived from and couched in identitive norms focused on conceptions of the 'nation' and 'national sovereignty'. Such assumptions, again, manifestly do not apply in the German case. The German state was characterised by Peter Katzenstein as 'semi-sovereign'.[1] Semi-sovereignty has two dimensions, internal and external. The internal dimension was the subject matter of Chapter 2. Here, it was shown that the German constitutional order diffuses and deconcentrates decision-making powers widely among central government departments, between federation and Länder, to 'parapublic' institutions such as the Bundesbank, and to a Constitutional Court which has made extremely active use of its powers to interpret and reshape the values and purposes embedded in the Basic Law. Policy-making within Germany is as a result, and more pervasively than in any other member state of the EU, a process involving perpetual negotiation among a wide range of institutional actors.

Amid the widening of the scope of European competence since the SEA, this internal dimension of semi-sovereignty has been extensively externalised, or Europeanised. Whereas the Federal Government – notwithstanding its traditional tendency to inter-departmental policy sectorisation – may have been able in the first two to three decades of European integration to claim and exercise a decision-making role in European policy essentially autonomous of the dispersed internal institutional structures of policy-making, this is no longer the case. Expanding European competence has confronted a much wider range of Federal Government departments with, and immersed them in, the European-level policy process. Expanding European competence has equally impinged increasingly on the internal policy remits of the Länder and the Bundesbank, leading them to claim and in large part secure access to relevant European policy communities. The implications of expanding European competence for the domestic constitutional order has, on occasion, and with its 1993 judgment on the TEU to an unprecedented degree, drawn the FCC into the European debate and caused it to set down markers to guide – and constrain – other German institutions in their engagement with 'Europe'. This was especially notable concerning the move to Stage III of EMU.

The cumulative result is that German European policy-making has, like domestic policy-making, become a process of managing institutional pluralism.[2] The process of negotiation and trade-off is both facilitated and complicated by the role played by political parties. Parties in one sense provide important linkages between different institutions, most notably on the federal–Länder dimension, that can lubricate the process of institutional consensus-building. They can also, and simultaneously, reinforce the points of potential institutional divergence within a sectorised Federal Government, in the Bundestag and within a federal system which, through the Bundesrat, can provide an additional channel of influence for those parties in opposition at the federal level. This can compound the problem of tactical weakness and incoherence of German European policy.

In a wider *strategic* sense, however, the large-scale consensus of the parties on the objectives of integration can have the effect of liberating and empowering governmental elites in the pursuit of German strategic goals. This can perhaps best be illustrated through comparison. The absence of party disagreement on the fundamentals of European policy in Germany, for example, presents a quite striking contrast to the situation in the UK, where inter-party differences and, in the Major era in particular, *intra-party* controversies over the strategic goals of European integration imposed weighty *constraints* on UK representatives in European-level negotiations. The paradox of tactical weakness and strategic empowerment is one developed further below (see pp. 131–2).

The external dimension of 'semi-sovereignty' has also been subject to important change in recent years. Its origins lay in the postwar settlement and the international politics of the Cold War. Constraints on sovereignty were in part imposed on the postwar Federal Republic, not least in the division of Germany, but also in the residual powers retained by the western occupying powers, which were subsequently reformulated in the context of the glaciation of the Cold War in the terms of West German membership of NATO. Constraints were also in part sought and accepted by the Adenauer governments in NATO and the early institutions of European integration as an exercise in good-neighbourliness, confidence-building, anti-Communism, rehabilitation and economic/trade regeneration. A core concern was to re-establish a workable relationship with France against the background of German aggression in 1870–71, 1914–18 and 1939–45.

These externally imposed and self-imposed constraints were remarkably successful, embedding West Germany in a network of multilateral relationships of an enduring character which laid much of the basis of West European peace, stability and prosperity in the postwar era. They were, though, in a sense, made redundant in 1989–90. The end of the Cold War removed some of the causes of constrained sovereignty at the same time as a newly unified Germany regained full control over its internal and external affairs in the 'Two plus Four' Treaty.

What had emerged in West Germany prior to unification and was confirmed after unification was, though, that a commitment to multilateralism in NATO and the EC/EU had embedded itself firmly as a *value* guiding German external policy. External semi-sovereignty had, notwithstanding the redundancy of the external postwar constraints, become deeply entrenched in a form of 'exaggerated' or 'reflexive' multilateralism which was accompanied by ambitious milieu goals of making the European policy environment even more multilateralist. All of the political institutions discussed above (see pp. 124–5), without exception,

Conclusions

had developed an attachment to the value of European integration robust enough to transcend, without serious challenge, the seismic changes in the international order of 1989–90. There has since been no regression to national interest politics (even assuming such an interest could coherently be defined given the institutional dispersal of decision-making power in Germany). Even in the controversy surrounding the recognition of Croatia, where Germany was confronted with accusations of a new national assertiveness, policy was made in the name of the principle of self-determination rather than of a German national interest. Though there is an emphasis under Schröder on identifying a clearer relation between national cost and benefit for Germany in EU matters, it still plays out against a background onto which Germany has continued to project a Europeanised identity – notwithstanding the reservations of an anxious public opinion – throughout the 1990s. The full implementation of EMU, further deepening through institutional reform and the realisation of eastern enlargement quite clearly remain as strategic goals to which Schröder and all other significant institutional actors unambiguously subscribe.

The projection of a Europeanised identity centred on multilateral cooperation requires partners, the subject of Chapter 3 of this study. The centrality here of the Franco–German partnership remains undimmed. Its postwar origins in the trade-off between French suspicions of German power and the German desire for rehabilitation and a stable trading climate have become deeply institutionalised. The level of co-ordination between France and Germany on European policy initiatives is unparalleled in the EU. It is the crucial nexus which facilitates important integration initiatives and around which wider decision-making coalitions at European level are built. The commitment on both sides of the relationship is deeply embedded even, as has been the case in recent years on aspects of institutional reform and eastern enlargement, where the two states diverge on specific issues of policy. Crucially, it has survived German unification and a change to France's disadvantage in the balance of adjustment. Indeed, it can plausibly be argued that the relationship has acted as a decompression chamber, allowing the French political elite to come to terms with Germany's increased political weight after unification.

All of Germany's other relationships have had a secondary character. The widening scope of European competence, especially where exercised under majority voting rules, together with the sheer gravity of recent, current and future initiatives on the Single Market, EMU, institutional reform and eastern enlargement, have, however, necessitated a purposeful widening of Germany's alliance strategy. This has not always been successful. The most successful example has probably been that of the German–Spanish relationship since Spanish accession in 1986, where common concerns to stabilise NATO's southern flank, a positive working relationship between Helmut Kohl and his counterpart for most of the intervening period, Felipé Gonzáles, and a conscious trade-off between market integration and cohesion policy combined to form a strong axis.[3] A counter-example would be the German–Italian relationship. This was important for much of the postwar period in sustaining the drive to integration. It was the sole relationship besides that with France to launch a number of EC-wide initiatives, such as the Genscher–Colombo 'European Act' of 1982. However, the German–Italian relationship was deeply affected by the centrality of EMU during the 1990s: Italy's participation in EMU was not a prospect regarded fondly by German policy-makers or public opinion and formed a major impetus behind the 'core Europe' debate of the mid-1990s and the negotiation of the Stability Pact in 1997–98. Here, public opinion was influential in the sense of requiring a sop to assuage its concerns on EMU in the form of a de-privileging of the formerly close German–Italian relationship.

Similarly, other examples of partnership-building and maintenance, including the ones chosen for analysis in this study, reveal a differentiated picture. The German–Dutch relationship provides a fascinating example of the reinvention of a relationship for a time weighed down by historical prejudice, poor personal relations and under-institutionalisation – despite large-scale convergence on the purposes of deeper integration and on specific policy issues. Personnel change and a stronger institutional underpinning designed to overcome the legacies of historical experience have transformed a lukewarm relationship into a positive one with a high degree of consensus on strategy which, importantly, gives Germany an access point to the loose caucus of smaller states sensitive about their role and influence in a growing and deepening union.

The German–British relationship proved, by contrast, not to be reinventable under John Major's premiership, despite a considerable area of overlap on particular fields of policy such as market integration, the EU budget and security issues. This reflected in part the constraints imposed by the privileged partnership with France. More generally, though, and despite a brief honeymoon period at the start of Major's Prime Ministership, the divergent politics of identity pursued by the two states prevented any convergence over the key issues that faced the EU, as was shown in the discussion of the IGC and EMU (pre-Blair) in Chapters 4 and 5. Under Major, the UK pursued with increasing emphasis, largely due to a highly divisive atmosphere of European policy debate within the governing party, a politics of national sovereignty quite incompatible with the multilateralist thrust of German policy. This prevented any fuller institutionalisation of the relationship, made even tactical cooperation on issues of shared concern increasingly difficult, and led to a German preference either for the institutional marginalisation of the UK within a union of flexible integration or a new negotiating partner in the form of a Labour government. The election of the latter under Tony Blair significantly improved UK–German relations and led to the almost unprecedented circumstance at Amsterdam of the German government opposing the introduction of QMV on policy areas where the new Labour government was in favour. The momentum has been maintained under the Schröder government, based on the ideological affinities he shared with Blair and broadly common interests in preparing the EU for enlargement. Nevertheless, Labour's conditional commitment to join the single currency – albeit not at the outset – places distinct limitations on UK–German relations becoming a core element of the integration over the short to medium term.

Reviewing the case studies

The purpose of bringing together the consideration of the internal institutional base for European policy-making alongside external alliance-building capacity was to allow, through detailed case-study analysis, an assessment of German power and effectiveness in the EU. It is useful, therefore, to draw together and compare the results of case-study Chapters 4–6 on the 1996–97 IGC, EMU and eastern enlargement. Table 7.1 presents an overview, revisiting the case studies according to common categories which facilitate comparison.

The first category points to the political context in which German EU diplomacy was engaged. Here, the IGC was distinctive, in that debate was focused in a tightly defined period which commenced with the appointment of the Commission's Reflection Group in June 1994, and was completed at the Amsterdam Summit in June 1997. It also had a clear if broad agenda, as set out in the treaty review process incorporated in the TEU and as fleshed out by the Reflection Group. Debates on both EMU and eastern enlargement extended across longer time periods, EMU from the Delors Report of 1988 through the TEU to the final date set out for Stage

Table 7.1 An overview of the case studies

Case study	Context	Domestic policy formulation	Partnership building	Milieu shaping
The 1996–97 IGC	• Short time period 1994–97 • Broad agenda set by Commission/Reflection Group	• Highly inclusive • No externalised veto points • Public opinion unconcerned	• Franco–German centrality, but unable to sustain agenda-setting • UK brokering role at Amsterdam	• Limited extension of multilateral policy cooperation
EMU	• Long time period, but 'big bang' in 1999 • Closed agenda rooted in the Maastricht Treaty's provisions on EMU	• Closed-policy community • Bundesbank/FCC position non-negotiable … • … and backed in public opinion	• Franco–German centrality … • … but buttressed by Dutch support on stability • UK Presidency facilitates Stage III	• Classic milieu shaping via explicit 'export' of German institutions and norms • Complementary concern of other member states to 'import' German monetary rigour
Eastern enlargement	• Long-term process without identifiable end-point • In the absence of a single documentary reference point, a very open agenda	• Highly inclusive • Periodic externalisation of sectorised policy positions … • … backed in key fields in public opinion	• Franco–German partnership difficult to sustain; post-Cold War balance of adjustment in Germany's favour overt • New alliance potentials with the UK, Netherlands and other northern states	• Traditional milieu shaping via extension of (geographical scope of) multilateral cooperation • 'Pre-emptive' institutional export via myriad institutional interactions

Conclusions 131

III on 1 January 1999, enlargement from the early 1990s through to some unspecified point of accession (for at least the first group of applicant states) in the 2000s. However, the blueprint for EMU established at Maastricht both for the EMU stability regime, and for the convergence criteria designed to sustain it, presented a tightly circumscribed policy agenda setting out conditions under which a once and for all 'big bang' transition to Stage III would take place. Enlargement has been both a more protracted process and more open-ended with no clear 'route map' or endpoint and with an agenda extending across the whole of the Union's *acquis* and beyond into wider geopolitical considerations.

These contextual differences set parameters in which domestic institutional interaction and external partnership capacities played out. Looking at domestic interaction first, it is worth recalling the discussion in Chapter 1 on Germany's institutional appearance as a multi-headed beast in European policy-making. This may result in significant tactical weaknesses in routine European policy-making, with German positions on particular policy issues relatively poorly coordinated across the institutions involved. It may also facilitate the attainment of strategic goals: there is a sense, discussed at length in Chapter 2, in which internal institutional positions may be externalised and presented as non-negotiable – or, at the very least, negotiable only at a high price. In our case studies, a variable picture emerged. Internal policy formulation for the IGC and the post-1997 enlargement debates was a very open process, touching on the institutional concerns of most Federal Government departments and the competences and/or territorial interests of the Länder. EMU policy formulation was by contrast much more closed. This reflected the more restricted circle of actors involved and the authority of the non-Federal Government actors which claimed a stake in the IGC negotiations: the Bundesbank and the FCC, arguably Germany's two most respected institutions internally and externally. The Federal Government could not diverge at all far from the conditions laid out by a central bank whose authority was an undisputed marker of monetary policy credibility within and without Germany. It also could not fail to take heed of the viewpoints presented by a Supreme Court which, as internal and external actors knew on the basis of its TEU judgment, had a capacity to explode the Maastricht timetable of the EMU project, or even, by throwing question marks over German participation, the project itself. In these circumstances, especially when a clearly engaged public opinion chimed with Bundesbank concerns, the Bundesbank/FCC position was very explicitly externalised to establish a non-negotiable German position on the quality of monetary stability to be attained by those wishing to join the Euro-zone.

In the IGC, German positions were for the most part relatively loose, broad aims, without the underlying common purpose among the core actors which produced the unconditionality of the German contribution to the EMU debate. And unlike EMU and, indeed, the pre-Maastricht IGCs, there were no domestic actors sufficiently concerned with the IGC agenda to be willing or able to impose potential veto positions on the Federal Government which might have been externalised onto Germany's partners. Equally, the IGC did not noticeably engage public opinion. As a result, no clear sense of a German end-game had emerged by the latter stages of the IGC, ostensibly leaving considerable room for manoeuvre in last-minute deal-making in the run-up to the Amsterdam Summit. However, at the last minute the changes of government in Britain and France, the disagreement on the eve of the European Council on stability versus employment and the overriding commitment to EMU conspired to produce a minimalist outcome, with Germany playing a much less pronounced strategic role than at Maastricht.

Enlargement has presented a middle position between EMU and the IGC. Amid a general consensus on Germany's strategic interest in enlargement, one or other of the many involved domestic actors has sought to establish veto positions: the Agriculture and Economics Ministries in the negotiations on the Europe Agreements; Agriculture again in the initial discussions on Agenda 2000 under Kohl; and the Finance Ministry under Schröder in particular on the budgetary aspects of Agenda 2000. This pattern is set to be repeated as the accession negotiations progressively cut across the 'possessions' of one or other of the federal ministries or concerns of particular interest to the Länder. It is not clear, though, that these internal constraints will allow the Federal Government – as with EMU – to shape the speed and direction of the process. The format of Agenda 2000 and in particular the accession negotiations, which address the *acquis* sequentially across policy areas, have created a large number of separate and in large part unconnected decision points – rather than EMU's big bang – less amenable to strategic direction, and more to reactive improvisation. German enlargement diplomacy will remain a form of 'yes, but ...' politics, with the 'buts' likely to emerge with growing frequency and force as accession nears. This is all the more the case in those areas where public concerns are strong enough to have electoral implications: on the EU budget, free movement of labour and border controls in particular.

The case studies also revealed a varied pattern of partnership relationships. As expected, the Franco–German relationship was consistently the most important. This was seen not least in the failure of the IGC to make real progress on preparing the EU institutionally for the enlargement era. While Franco–German agenda-setting made much of the running in the early phases of the IGC, the complications raised at the death by the new Jospin government diverted the impetus away from institutional reform into trade-offs over EMU. The result – institutional non-reform – was indicative of how Franco–German agreement is a prerequisite for treaty reform. On EMU, Franco–German agreement had always been at the heart of the project. And despite a number of 'wobbles' on the trade-off between monetary and employment policy, especially under Jospin, this agreement survived to act as the mainstay for the launch of EMU in 1999. Significantly, though, German investment in a more fully institutionalised relationship with the Netherlands paid back in the form of a further, authoritative voice pushing a German-style stability agenda, in particular in stiffening the resolution of southern member states in meeting the Maastricht criteria.

In neither of these cases – nor in enlargement policy – did the relationship with the UK pre-Blair prove useful in pursuing German strategic aims. The fragility and unreliability of the Major government's commitment to the EU placed the UK at the periphery of Germany's alliance strategy. There has been a significant change since the election of the Blair government, with Blair helping to mediate between France and Germany at the end of the IGC, and providing a robust and positive framework for the final decisions on Euro-zone membership taken during the British Presidency in 1998. The development of the Blair–Schröder relationship, rooted in a vision of modernised Social Democracy, has since provided important ballast. This relaunched partnership, now undergoing fuller institutionalisation, almost produced a powerful alliance on budget and CAP reform on Agenda 2000. The foundations of that alliance remain in place, though, and have begun to qualify the 'exclusivity' once invested into the Franco–German relationship. Even before Schröder, there were obvious difficulties in sustaining Franco–German common purpose on enlargement given that it implied a rebalancing of the EU away from a France-centred west/south European core and towards a German-centred north-east. The sense of rebalancing was intensified by the bitterness of the debate in Agenda 2000 over CAP and budget reform, where French and German positions were scarcely reconcilable. German commonalities on Agenda 2000 with the

Netherlands and others also suggest a greater fluidity in German alliance strategies in the future.

How far, finally, do the three case studies reveal a milieu-shaping Germany? On the IGC, not very much if one looks beyond the fuller embedding of the second and third pillars in the integration project. The absence of clear institutional veto positions, such as the Länder and the Bundesbank presented at Maastricht, and of a shared Franco–German vision capable of transcending the change of government at the end of the IGC produced a minimalist outcome. EMU presents a vastly different picture. The continued externalisation of non-negotiable Bundesbank positions (and, in large part their enthusiastic acceptance by other member states such as the Netherlands), plus the maintenance of Franco–German unity despite a number of passing difficulties, allowed the EMU project against many expectations to enter its final stage. And it has done so very explicitly as the German template agreed at Maastricht and buttressed further down the line by the Stability Pact. Enlargement presents a somewhat different, though also extremely important, picture of milieu shaping. In one sense, this is consistent with the received thrust of German strategies of multilateralising the regional milieu in Europe; enlargement will extend the area in which the multilateral *aquis* Germany has established with its partners since the 1950s applies. There is also, though, a second thrust of milieu shaping which reflects the essentially sectorised nature of the enlargement process, and which deals separately with different policy areas. This process has encouraged myriad German actors to engage with their counterparts in the accession states and to diffuse institutional and policy know-how into the German 'near-abroad'. In other words, CEE is becoming more 'German' *before* enlargement. The implications for the disposition of German power after enlargement are clear.

German power

Our final point is to return, on this note, to the faces of power outlined in our introduction. Germany's European diplomacy, as has been argued, does not centre on the pursuit of realist power. German power in the EU is not the product of a centrally-steered policy by government nor just of German size and geographical centrality. It is, rather, a combination of an influential vision, valuable institutional models to export to the EU, a solid domestic political consensus and an important set of bilateral relationships. Moreover, Germany's main source of 'unintentional power' – that of the Bundesbank's international weight and influence – is being progressively reined in as EMU takes shape. However, by the same process, the Bundesbank's unintentional power is being recast as a form of indirect institutional power, as its monetary policy norms are 'exported' into the framework for EMU governance. This process is reinforced by the other forms of 'institutional export' noted in Chapter 2: the role of the Länder in shaping European-level institutions in the TEU and their redrafting of Article 23 of the Basic Law, and the implications of the Constitutional Court's TEU judgment for the interpretation of the new Article 23 and the move towards EMU. The process of approximation of domestic German and European structures of government is thus set to continue.

More broadly, the continuing commitment of Germany's European policy-makers to seek multilateral European solutions to contemporary political problems will continue to entrench at the European level a style of cooperative, consensus-orientated decision-making comparable to that which exists in Germany, and with which German actors are familiar and comfortable. This helps to complete the virtuous circle – noted in our introduction – in which indirect institutional power is influential for the configuration of European institutions and the style of their interactions, and subsequently 'pays back' through systemic empowerment. This process is set to be accelerated once the applicant states in CEE, already subject to penetration by German norms, accede to the EU in the 2000s. In this sense, the polarisation of prognoses noted at the outset of this book about whether a 'European Germany' or a 'German Europe' is emerging is a false dichotomy. Both prognoses are in a sense true, as a Europeanised Germany continues to make its distinctive mark on the institutional character of the EU.

Notes

1 P. Katzenstein, *Policy and Politics in West Germany: The Growth of a Semi-Sovereign State* (Philadelphia: Temple University Press, 1987).
2 This had become clearly evident by the mid-1980s, forming, for example, a core theme in Bulmer and Paterson, *The Federal Republic of Germany and the European Community*, written in 1986.
3 Relations between Germany and Spain were however tested greatly in the context of the Agenda 2000 negotiations where Germany's budgetary concerns and Spain's commitment to retain the benefits of the Cohesion Fund were unbridgeable. While Germany backed down in 1999 under the pressures of the Presidency, this is a difference of interest which will no doubt re-emerge.

Select bibliography

Anderson, J., *German Unification and the Union of Europe: The Domestic Politics of Integration Policy* (Cambridge: Cambridge University Press, 1999).
Anderson, J., 'Hard Interests, Soft Power, and Germany's Changing Role in Europe', in P. Katzenstein (ed.), *Tamed Power: Germany in Europe* (Ithaca, NY: Cornell University Press, 1997).
Anderson, J. and J. Goodman, 'Mars or Minerva? A United Germany in a Post-Cold War Europe', in R. O. Keohane, J. S. Nye and S. Hoffmann (eds), *After the Cold War: International Institutions and State Strategies in Europe, 1989–1991* (Cambridge, MA: Harvard University Press, 1993).
Andreae, L. and K. Kaiser, 'Die "Außenpolitik" der Fachministerien', in W. Eberwein and K. Kaiser (eds), *Deutschlands neue Außenpolitik. Band 4: Institutionen und Ressourcen* (Munich: Oldenbourg, 1998).
Armstrong, K. and S. Bulmer, 'The United Kingdom', in D. Rometsch and W. Wessels (eds), *The European Union and Member States: Towards Institutional Fusion?* (Manchester: Manchester University Press, 1996).
Birgelen, G., 'Europapolitische Meinungsbildung in Deutschland', in W. Weidenfeld (ed.), *Deutsche Europapolitik* (Bonn: Europa Union Verlag, 1998).
Blair, T. and G. Schröder, 'Europe: The Third Way/Die Neue Mitte', http://www.labour.org.uk/views/items/00000053.html (1999).
Blume, G. and A. Graf von Rex, 'Weiterentwicklung der inhaltlichen und personellen Mitwirkung der Länder in Angelegenheiten der EU nach Maastricht', in F. Borkenhagen (ed.), *Europapolitik der deutschen Länder. Bilanz und Perspektiven nach dem Gipfel von Amsterdam* (Opladen: Leske und Budrich, 1998).
Buller, J. and C. Jeffery, 'Britain, Germany and the Deepening of Europe', in K. Larres and E. Meehan (eds), *Uneasy Allies: British–German Relations and European Integration Since 1945* (Oxford: Oxford University Press, 2000).
Bulmer, S., 'Shaping the Rules? The Constitutive Politics of the European Union and German Power', in P. Katzenstein (ed.), *Tamed Power: Germany in Europe* (Ithaca, NY: Cornell University Press, 1997).

Bulmer, S. and M. Burch, 'Maastricht II und danach: Großbritannien doch am Herzen Europas?', *Wirtschaftsdienst*, 12 (1998).

Bulmer, S. and W. Paterson, *The Federal Republic of Germany and the European Community* (London: Allen & Unwin, 1987).

Bulmer, S. and W. Paterson, 'European Policy-Making in the Federal Republic: Internal and External Limits to Leadership', in W. Wessels and E. Regelsberger (eds), *The Federal Republic of Germany and the European Community: The Presidency and Beyond* (Bonn: Europa Union Verlag, 1987).

Burley, A-M., 'Regulating the World: Multilateralism, International Law and the Projection of the New Deal Regulatory State', in J. G. Ruggie (ed.), *Multilateralism Matters: The Theory and Praxis of an Institutional Form* (New York: Columbia University Press, 1993).

Busse, V., 'Regierungsbildung aus organisatorischer Sicht. Tatsächliche und rechtliche Betrachtungen am Beispiel des Regierungswechsels 1998', *Die Öffentliche Verwaltung*, 52 (1999).

Collins, S., 'Managing the Agenda? German Policy-Making with Regard to Eastern Enlargement of the European Union', Ph.D. dissertation, Institute for German Studies, University of Birmingham, 1999.

Conversi, D., 'German-Bashing and the Breakup of Yugoslavia', *The Donald W. Treadgold Papers in Russian, East European and Central Asian Studies*, No. 16, University of Washington (1998).

Crawford, B., 'German Foreign Policy and European Political Cooperation: the Diplomatic Recognition of Croatia in 1991', *German Politics and Society*, 13 (Summer 1995).

de la Serre, F. and C. Lequesne, 'Frankreich', in W. Weidenfeld and W. Wessels (eds), *Jahrbuch der Europäischen Integration 1996/97* (Bonn: Europa Union Verlag, 1998).

de la Serre, F. and C. Lequesne, 'Frankreich', in W. Weidenfeld and W. Wessels (eds), *Jahrbuch der Europäischen Integration 1997/98* (Bonn: Europa Union Verlag, 1999).

Deubner, C., 'Frankreich in der Osterweiterung der EU, 1989 bis 1997', *Politische Studien*, 50 (1999).

Deubner, C. and J. Janning, 'Zur Reform des Abstimmungsverfahrens im Rat der EU. Überlegungen und Modellrechnungen, ausgehend von einer Veränderung der Stimmgewichtung', *Stiftung Wissenschaft und Politik*, SWP-IP 2971 (September 1996).

Diekmann, K. and R. Reuth, *Helmut Kohl: Ich wollte Deutschlands Einheit* (Berlin: Propyläen, 1996).

Dyson, K. and K. Featherstone, 'EMU and Economic Governance in Germany', *German Politics*, 5 (1996).

Dyson, K., *Elusive Union: The Process of Economic and Monetary Union in Europe* (Harlow: Longman, 1994).

Edwards, G. and A. Pijpers (eds), *The Politics of European Treaty Reform. The 1996 Intergovernmental Conference and Beyond* (London: Pinter, 1997).

Fischer, W., 'Von Maastricht nach Amsterdam. Die Regierungskonferenz aus Sicht der deutschen Länder', *Zeitschrift für Parlamentsfragen*, 29 (1998).
Garton-Ash, T., 'Germany's Choice', *Foreign Affairs*, 73 (1994).
Goetz, K., 'Integration Policy in a Europeanised State: Germany and the Intergovernmental Conference', *Journal of European Public Policy*, 3 (1996).
Guzzini, S., 'Structural Power: The Limits of Neorealist Power Analysis', *International Organisation*, 47 (Summer 1993).
Hahn, O., 'EG-Engagement der Länder: Lobbyismus oder Nebenaußenpolitik?', in R. Hrbek and U. Thaysen (eds), *Die deutschen Länder und die Europäischen Gemeinschaften* (Baden-Baden: Nomos, 1986).
Hayward, J., 'Britain and EU Enlargement', in K. Kaiser and M. Brüning (eds), *East-Central Europe and the EU: Problems of Integration* (Bonn: Europa Union Verlag, 1996).
Hellmann, G., 'Nationale Normalität als Zukunft? Zur Außenpolitik der Berliner Republik', in *Blätter für deutsche und internationale Politik*, 24 (1999).
Herdegen, M., 'After the TV Judgement of the German Constitutional Court: Decison-making within the EU Council and the German Länder', *Common Market Law Review*, 32 (1995).
Hesse, J. and M. Schaad, 'Leapfrogging, Side-Stepping or Paradise Lost? Amsterdam and the European Union', *Staatswissenschaften und Staatspraxis*, 9 (1998).
Hort, P., 'Wird die Europapolitik britischer?', *Frankfurter Allgemeine Zeitung*, 30 October 1997.
Hrbek, R., 'Eine politische Bewertung der VW-Beihilfen-Kontroverse', *Wirtschaftsdienst*, 10 (1996).
Institut für Europäische Politik (ed.), *Enlargement/Agenda 2000 Watch*, Pilot Issue (October 1998).
Istituto Affari Internazionali, *Revision of Maastricht. Implementation and Proposals for Reform. A Survey of National Views*, Fifth Bulletin (January–June 1996).
Janning, J., 'Bundesrepublik Deutschland', in W. Weidenfeld and W. Wessels (eds), *Jahrbuch der Europäischen Integration 1996/97* (Bonn: Europa Union Verlag, 1998).
Janning, J., 'Bundesrepublik Deutschland', in W. Weidenfeld and W. Wessels (eds), *Jahrbuch der Europäischen Integration 1997/98* (Bonn: Europa Union Verlag, 1999).
Jansen, L., *Bekend en onbemind. Het beeld van Duitsland en Duitsers onder jongeren van vijftien tot negentien jaar* (Den Haag: Instituut Clingendael, 1993).
Jeffery, C., 'Sub-National Mobilisation and European Integration. Does it Make a Difference?', *Journal of Common Market Studies*, 38 (2000).
Jeffery, C., 'The German Länder and the "Normalisation" of the EU Enlargement Debate', *Zentrum für Europäische Integrationsforschung, Bonn, Discussion Papers* (2000).
Jeffery, C., 'Les Länder allemands et l'Europe: intérêts, stratégies et influence dans les politiques communautaires', in E. Negrier and B. Jouve (eds), *Que gouvernent les regions d'Europe* (Paris: L'Harmattan, 1998).

Jeffery, C., 'Britische Positionen zur Regierungskonferenz 1996 – Ein Wandel in Sicht?', in *Maastricht II – Zum Erfolg verurteilt?* (Erfurt: Schriftenreihe des Thüringer Ministeriums für Justiz und Europaangelegenheiten, 1996).
Jeffery, C., 'Farewell the Third Level? The German Länder and the European Policy Process', *Regional and Federal Studies*, 6 (1996).
Jeffery, C., 'A Giant with Feet of Clay? United Germany in the European Union', *University of Birmingham Discussion Papers in German Studies*, No. IGS95/6 (1995).
Jeffery, C., 'The German Länder and the 1996 Intergovernmental Conference', *Regional and Federal Studies*, 5 (1995).
Jeffery, C., 'The Länder Strike Back: Structures and Procedures of European Integration Policy-Making in the German Federal System', *Leicester University Discussion Papers in Federal Studies*, No. FS94/4 (1994).
Jeffery, C., 'Plus ça Change ... The Non-Reform of the German Federal System after Unification', *Leicester University Discussion Papers in Federal Studies*, No. FS93/2 (1993).
Jeffery, C. and S. Collins, 'The German Länder and EU Enlargement: Between Apple Pie and Issue Linkage', *German Politics*, 7 (1998).
Jeffery, C. and V. Handl, 'Germany and Europe after Kohl: Between Social Democracy and Normalisation?', *Birmingham One Europe Discussion Papers* (2000).
Jeffery, C. and V. Handl, 'Blair, Schröder and the Third Way', in L. Funk (ed.), *The Economics and Politics of the Third Way* (Hamburg: LIT-Verlag, 1999).
Jessen, C., 'Agenda 2000: Das Reformpaket von Berlin, ein Erfolg für Gesamteuropa', *Integration*, 22 (1999).
Jopp, M., 'Germany and EU Enlargement', in K. Kaiser and M. Brüning (eds), *East-Central Europe and the EU: Problems of Integration* (Bonn: Europa Union Verlag, 1996).
Jopp, M. and O. Schmuck (eds), *Die Reform der Europäischen Union. Analysen – Positionen – Dokumente zur Regierungskonferenz 1996/97* (Bonn: Europa Union Verlag, 1996).
Kaiser, K. and M. Brüning (eds), *East-Central Europe and the EU: Problems of Integration* (Bonn: Europa Union Verlag, 1996).
Kaiser, K. and J. Roper, *British–German Defence Cooperation: Partners within the Alliance* (London: Royal Institute of International Affairs, 1988).
Kalbfleisch-Kottsieper, U., 'Fortentwicklung des Föderalismus in Europa – vom Provinzialismus zur stabilen politischen Perspektive?', *Die Öffentliche Verwaltung*, 46 (1993).
Karpenstein, U., 'Der Vertrag von Amsterdam im Lichte der Maastricht-Entscheidung des BVerfG', *Deutsches Verwaltungsblatt*, 17 (1998).
Katzenstein, P., 'Germany and Mitteleuropa', in P. Katzenstein (ed.), *Mitteleuropa. Between Europe and Germany* (Oxford: Berghahn, 1997).
Katzenstein, P., *Policy and Politics in West Germany: The Growth of a Semi-Sovereign State* (Philadelphia: Temple University Press, 1987).

Katzenstein, P. (ed.), *Between Power and Plenty: Foreign Economic Policies of Advanced Industrial States* (Madison: University of Wisconsin Press, 1978).

Keatinge, P. and A. Murphy, 'The European Council's Ad Hoc Committee on Institutional Affairs (1984–85)', in R. Pryce (ed.), *The Dynamics of European Union* (Beckenham: Croom Helm, 1987).

Kerremans B. and J. Beyers, 'The Belgian Subnational Entities in the European Union: "Second" or "Third Level" Players', *Regional and Federal Studies*, 6 (1996).

Kielinger, T., 'Anglo-German Relationships within Wider Partnerships', speech delivered at Royal United Services Institute/Stiftung Wissenschaft und Politik Conference, Ebenhausen, 28 June 1996.

Klär, K., *Reformen für ein bürgernahes Europa. Die Regierungskonferenz 1996*, 2nd edn (Bonn: Rheinland-Pfalz, 1996).

Klein, Y., 'Obstructive or Promoting? British Views on German Unification 1989/90', *German Politics*, 5 (1996).

Koch, K., 'The Netherlands and EU Enlargement', in K. Kaiser and M. Brüning (eds), *East-Central Europe and the EU: Problems of Integration* (Bonn: Europa Union Verlag, 1996).

Kohl, H., *Our Future in Europe* (Edinburgh/London, Europa Institute/Konrad Adenauer Foundation, 1991).

Kreile, M., 'West Germany: The Dynamics of Expansion', in P. Katzenstein (ed.), *Between Power and Plenty: Foreign Economic Policies of Advanced Industrial States* (Madison: University of Wisconsin Press, 1978).

Kwast-van Duursen, M., 'Niederlande', in W. Weidenfeld and W. Wessels (eds), *Jahrbuch der Europäischen Integration 1995/96* (Bonn: Europa Union Verlag, 1997).

Laffan, B., '"While you're there in Brussels, Get us a Grant." The Management of the Structural Funds in Ireland', *Irish Political Studies*, 4 (1989).

Lafontaine, O. and D. Strauss-Kahn, 'Europa – sozial und stark. Märkte brauchen die ordnende Hand des Staates', *Die Zeit*, No. 3 (1999).

Langguth, G., 'Ein sozialistisches Europa? Ist die These "vom Ende des sozialdemokratischen Jahrhunderts" widerlegt?', *Politische Studien*, 50 (1999).

Le Gloannec, A-M., 'The Purpose of German Power', in Z. Laïki (ed.), *Power and Purpose after the Cold War* (Providence: Berg Publishers).

Lippert, B., 'Die Erweiterungspolitik der Europäischen Union', in W. Weidenfeld and W. Wessels (eds), *Jahrbuch der Europäischen Integration 1997/98* (Bonn: Europa Union Verlag, 1999).

Lippert, B., 'Der Gipfel von Luxemburg: Startschuß für das Abenteuer Erweiterung', *Integration*, 21 (1998).

Lukes, S., *Power: A Radical View* (London: Macmillan, 1974).

Maier, C., 'The Politics of Productivity: Foundations of American International Economic Policy After World War II', in P. Katzenstein (ed.), *Between Power and Plenty: Foreign Economic Policies of Advanced Industrial States* (Madison: University of Wisconsin Press, 1978).

Marsh, D., *The Germans: Rich, Bothered and Divided* (London: Century, 1989).

Marsh, D., *The Bundesbank: The Bank that Rules Europe* (London: Mandarin, 1993).

McCarthy, P., 'France, Germany, the IGC and Eastern Enlargement', in D. Webber (ed.), *The Franco–German Relationship in the European Union* (London: Routledge, 1999).

Nicholls, A., 'Germany and the European Union: Has Unification Altered Germany's European Policy?', *International House of Japan Bulletin*, 14 (1994).

Noelle-Neumann, E. and T. Petersen, 'Die öffentliche Meinung', in W. Weidenfeld and W. Wessels (eds), *Jahrbuch der Europäischen Integration 1997/98* (Bonn: Europa Union Verlag, 1999).

Oschatz, G-B. and H. Risse, 'Die Bundesregierung an der Kette der Länder? Zur europapolitischen Mitwirkung des Bundesrates', *Die Öffentliche Verwaltung*, 48 (1995).

Paterson, W., 'Beyond Semi-Sovereignty: The New Germany in the New Europe', *German Politics*, 5 (1996).

Paterson, W., 'The Chancellor and Foreign Policy', in S. Padgett (ed.), *Adenauer to Kohl: The Development of the German Chancellorship* (London: Hurst, 1994).

Paterson, W. and C. Jeffery, *Großbritannien nach dem Machtwechsel: New Labour, Devolution und Europapolitik* (St. Augustin: Konrad-Adenauer-Stiftung Arbeitspapiere, 1997).

Paterson, W., 'Helmut Kohl, "The Vision Thing" and Escaping the Semi-Sovereignty Trap', in C. Clemens and W. E. Paterson (eds), *The Kohl Chancellorship* (London: Frank Cass, 1998).

Pflüger, F., 'Europa muß Weltmacht werden. Weichenstellungen der deutschen Ratspräsidentschaft', *Internationale Politik* (1999).

Pijpers, A. and J. Rood, 'Niederlande', in W. Weidenfeld and W. Wessels (eds), *Jahrbuch der Europäischen Integration 1997/98* (Bonn: Europa Union Verlag, 1999).

Pijpers, A. and S. Vanhoonacker, 'The Position of the Benelux Countries', in G. Edwards and A. Pijpers (eds), *The Politics of European Treaty Reform. The 1996 Intergovernmental Conference and Beyond* (London: Pinter, 1997).

Proudfoot, N., *Europeanisation and the New Regionalism. The Case of Bavaria*, M.Phil. dissertation, University of Cambridge (1997).

Putnam, R., 'Diplomacy and Domestic Politics: The Logic of Two Level Games', *International Organisation*, 42 (1989).

Regelsberger, E. and W. Wessels, 'National Paper on the Federal Republic of Germany', in C. O. Nuallain, *The Presidency of the European Council of Ministers* (London: Croom Helm, 1985).

Reinhardt, N., 'A Turning Point in the German EMU Debate: The Baden-Württemberg Regional Election of March 1996', *German Politics*, 6 (1997).

Ress, G., 'The Constitution and the Maastricht Treaty: Between Cooperation and Conflict', *German Politics*, 3 (1994).

Sbragia, A., 'Environmental Policy: the "Push-Pull" of Policy-Making', in

H. Wallace and W. Wallace (eds), *Policy-Making in the European Union*, 3rd edn (Oxford: Oxford University Press, 1996).

Schmuck, O., 'Die EU-Regierungskonferenz 1996: Zum Stand der Reformdebatte', *Integration* 18 April 1995.

Sedelmeier, U., 'The European Union's Association Policy Towards Central and Eastern Europe', *Sussex European Institute Discussion Paper* (1994).

Simonian, H., *The Privileged Partnership: Franco–German Relations in the European Community 1969–84* (Oxford: Oxford University Press, 1985).

Singer, M. and A. Wildavsky, *The Real World Order. Zones of Peace, Zones of Turmoil* (Chatham: Chatham House Publishers, 1996).

Smeets, H-D., 'Does Germany Dominate the EMS?', *Journal of Common Market Studies*, 29 January 1990.

Sperling, J., 'German Foreign Policy after Unification: The End of Cheque Book Diplomacy', *West European Politics*, 17 (1994).

Stephenson, J., 'Anniversaries, Memory and Neighbours. The German Question in Recent History', *German Politics*, 5 (1996).

Stubb, A., 'The 1996 Intergovernmental Conference and the Management of Flexible Integration', *Journal of European Public Policy*, 4 (1997).

Szukala, A. and W. Wessels, 'The Franco-German Tandem', in G. Edwards and A. Pijpers (eds), *The Politics of European Treaty Reform. The 1996 Intergovernmental Conference Beyond* (London: Pinter, 1997).

Teilungsfolgen. Materialsammlung zum Streit um staatliche Beihilfe an die Volkswagen AG für ein Investitionsvorhaben im Freistaat Sachsen (Dresden: Sächsische Staatskanzlei, 1996).

Tewes, H., 'Germany as a Civilian Power. The Western Integration of East Central Europe', Ph.D. dissertation, Institute for German Studies, University of Birmingham, 1999.

Tewes, H., 'Between Deepening and Widening: Role Conflict in Germany's Enlargement Policy', *West European Politics*, 21 (1998).

Thatcher, M., *The Downing Street Years* (London: Harper Collins, 1993).

Unterwedde, H., 'Deutsch-Französische Beziehungen: Perspektiven einer spannungsgeladenen Partnerschaft', *Politische Studien*, 49 (1998).

van Traa, M., 'Wohlbekannt aber ungeliebt? Der deutsche Nachbar aus niederländischer Sicht', *Europa-Archiv* (1994).

Wallace, H., 'Foreign Policy. The Management of Distinctive Interests', in R. Morgan and C. Bray (eds), *Partners and Rivals in Western Europe* (London: 1986).

Wallace, W., 'Germany as Europe's Leading Power', *The World Today* (1995).

Weidenfeld, W. (ed.), *Deutsche Europapolitik: Optionen wirksamer Interessenvertretung* (Bonn: Europa Union Verlag, 1998).

Weidenfeld, W. and W. Wessels (eds), *Jahrbuch der Europäischen Integration 1997/98* (Bonn: Europa Union Verlag, 1999).

Weidenfeld, W. and W. Wessels (eds), *Jahrbuch der Europäischen Integration 1996/97* (Bonn: Europa Union Verlag, 1998).

Weidenfeld, W. and W. Wessels (eds), *Jahrbuch der Europäischen Integration*

1995/96 (Bonn: Europa Union Verlag, 1997).

Weiler, J., 'Fin de Siècle Europe', in R. Dehousse (ed.), *Europe after Maastricht: An ever Closer Union?* (Munich: Löbe, 1994).

Wessels, W. and D. Rometsch, 'German Administrative Interaction and European Union: The Fusion of Public Policies', in Y. Mény and P. Muller, J-L. Quermonne (eds), *Adjusting to Europe. The Impact of the European Union on National Institutions and Policies* (London: Routledge, 1996).

Westlake, M., 'Keynote Article: "Mad Cows and Englishmen" – The International Consequences of the BSE Crisis', *The European Union 1996: Annual Review of Activities, Journal of Common Market Studies*, 35 (special issue) (1997).

Wincott, D., 'Human Rights, Democracy and the Role of the Court of Justice in European Integration', *Democratisation*, 1 (1994).

Wolfers, A., *Discord and Collaboration* (Baltimore: Johns Hopkins, 1962).

Zelikow, P. and C. Rice, *Germany Unified and Europe Transformed* (Cambridge, MA: Harvard University Press, 1995).

Index

Acquis Communautaire 17, 77, 105, 118, 131, 132, 134
Adenauer, K. 3, 23, 52, 55, 56, 126
Amsterdam Treaty/Summit 3, 11, 14, 16, 58, 68, 76–89, 100, 116, 129, 130, 132
Andreotti, G. 61
Austria 69, 78

Baden-Württemberg 36, 38, 95, 96, 98
Bahr, E. 33
Basic Law 2, 22, 34, 38–40, 42–44, 46, 81, 83, 97, 125, 135
Basle-Nyborg Agreement 15
Bavaria 36–8, 81, 93, 96, 98, 108, 112, 113
Behrendt, R. 37
Belgium 35, 61, 86, 98, 116
Biedenkopf, K. 93, 98
Bitterlich, J. 68, 69
Blair, T. 6, 7, 11, 14, 32, 54, 59, 60, 64, 68–70, 73, 78, 83, 86, 88, 102, 119, 129, 133
Blair–Schröder paper 32, 69, 70
Borchert, J. 79
Bremen 36
British Beef/BSE 4, 6, 11, 16, 67, 87
Broek, H. van den 61, 63
Brown, G. 32

Brunner, M. 44, 95
Bund Freier Bürger 95
Bundesbank 11, 12, 14, 15, 22, 26, 27, 40–2, 46, 67, 71, 72, 92–4, 96–100, 124, 125, 130, 131, 134, 135
Bundesrat 24, 34, 35, 37, 39, 40, 43, 81, 82, 93, 96, 98, 125
Bundestag 24, 44–6, 96–8, 125

CDU 26, 27, 29–32, 80, 96, 98, 109
Chirac, J. 58, 59, 84, 85, 100
City of London 65, 66
Cohesion Fund 110, 111, 128
Cold War 1, 2, 4, 7, 104, 105, 115, 118, 126
Committee of Permanent Representatives (COREPER) 28, 35
Committee of the Regions 33, 34, 41, 81–3
Common Agricultural Policy (CAP) 17, 26, 44, 55, 57, 59, 76, 80, 107–12, 117–19, 133
Common Foreign and Security Policy (CFSP) 8, 24, 34, 62, 77, 85–7
Conservative Party 64–8, 87
Cook, R. 32, 88
Council of Ministers 12, 22, 23, 28, 31, 34, 39, 41, 56, 77, 79, 132

Index

Council of Environment Ministers 26
Council of Finance Ministers (ECOFIN) 61
Council of Foreign Ministers 61
Croatia 6, 30, 61, 62, 127
CSU 26, 27, 29–32, 80, 93, 96, 108, 109
Cyprus 104
Czech Republic 38, 104, 113
Czechoslovakia 104

Daimler-Benz 59
Dankert, P. 61, 62
De Charette, H. 85
De Gaulle, C. 53
Dehaene, J. 62
Delors Committee on EMU 41, 57, 94
Delors, J. 53, 56, 62, 64
Denmark 54, 67, 77
Deutsche Bank 59
Deutschmark (DM) 4, 10, 14, 15, 41, 92, 95, 115
Duisenberg, W. 63, 64, 100, 101

Eastern Enlargement 3, 8, 10, 12, 17, 18, 25, 27, 30, 32, 38, 54, 59, 73, 76, 80, 84, 104–20, 127–34
Economic and Monetary Union (EMU) 1–4, 6, 8, 10–12, 14–18, 23, 24, 26, 29–31, 41, 42, 45, 46, 57–61, 63, 65, 66, 68, 69, 71, 73, 76–8, 80–2, 84–9, 92–102, 106, 108, 110, 115, 116, 125, 127, 129–35
EFTA 12
Eling, L. 66
Estonia 104
EU Budget 6, 12, 17, 18, 24, 73, 76, 104, 107–11, 117–19, 128, 132, 133
European Central Bank (ECB) 12, 14, 41, 45, 52, 63, 66, 92, 94, 95, 100, 101, 116

European Coal and Steel Community 1, 24
European Commission 27, 38, 53, 62, 77, 87, 98, 104, 108, 110–12, 130
European Council (Rome, 1990) 31, 79, 80, 104, 105, 110, 111, 117
European Court of Justice 44, 45
European Defence Community 55
European Monetary Institute 94
European Monetary System (EMS) 12, 14, 15, 41, 56
European Parliament 11, 12, 71, 77, 84, 87, 96
European People's Party (EPP) 31
European Political Union 1, 41, 42, 57, 65, 71, 84, 85, 93
Exchange Rate Mechanism (ERM) 4, 15, 41, 66, 67, 72

Falconer, Lord 32
FDP 26, 29, 30, 80
Federal Constitutional Court (FCC) 11, 22, 44–6, 92, 94, 96–9, 124, 125, 130, 131, 135
Federal Government
  Agricultural Ministry 26, 27, 107, 109, 132
  Chancellor's Office 23, 25, 93, 106, 107
  Economics Ministry 23–7, 36, 79, 93, 106, 107, 110,
  Environment Ministry 26, 27, 79
  Federal Affairs Ministry 36
  Finance Ministry 24–7, 36, 79, 93, 101, 108, 110, 111, 132
  Food, Agriculture & Forestry Ministry 26
  Foreign Office 23–6, 29, 36, 79, 81, 83, 93, 106, 107, 114
  Interior Ministry 26, 27, 36, 79, 113
  Justice Ministry 26, 36
Finland 78
Fischer, J. 10, 25, 29, 30, 59, 69

'Flexibility' 77, 78, 80, 85–8, 116
Fouchet Plan 53
France Telecom 100
France 2, 10–12, 15, 18, 26, 28, 31, 52– 60, 62, 64, 68–73, 78, 80, 84–6, 97–102, 105, 106, 109–111, 114– 19, 126–28, 132, 133
Franco–German Relations 3, 11, 23, 24, 30, 53–60, 62–4, 67, 69–72, 84–8, 99–101, 105, 114–17, 120, 127, 130, 133, 134
Friedrich Ebert Foundation 32

Genscher, H. 12, 30, 61, 105
German–Dutch Relations 54, 60–4, 72, 73, 86, 87, 101, 118, 128, 133
German Farmers Union (*Deutscher Bauernverband*) 26
German–Italian Relations 128
German–Polish Relations 54
German–Spanish Relations 128
German Unification 1, 2, 4, 8, 15, 23, 27, 40, 53, 60, 61, 64, 65, 70, 92, 99, 126, 127
Giscard d'Estaing, V. 56, 100
Gonzáles, F. 128
Green Party 8, 10, 26, 28–30, 80, 95, 109

Herzog, R. 63
Hesse 36
Hombach, B. 32
Hoyerswerda 62
Hungary 104, 117
Hurd, D. 5

Intergovernmental Conference (IGC – 1990–91) 31, 40, 41
Intergovernmental Conference (IGC – 1996–97) 10, 11, 17, 18, 31, 38, 41, 46, 57, 63, 73, 76–89, 92, 106, 116, 129, 132–34
Ireland 78

Italy 12, 15, 95, 98, 101, 116

Jospin, L. 58, 69, 78, 81, 83, 86, 88, 133
Justice and Home Affairs (JHA) 12, 14, 16, 26, 77, 85–8

Kinkel, K. 29, 85
Kirchhof, P. 96, 97
Kohl, H. 1, 3, 8, 10–12, 14, 18, 23, 24, 26, 30–3, 38, 42, 53, 56–8, 61–6, 68, 71, 80, 83–8, 96, 98–100, 105, 106, 108–11, 113, 117, 128, 132
Kok, W. 61, 63
Konrad Adenauer Foundation 32
Kooijmans, P. 63
Kosovo Conflict 5, 8, 110

Labour Party 31, 32, 68, 70, 88, 129
Lafontaine, O. 4, 25, 58, 69, 70, 95, 100, 101
Lamers, K. 32, 33
Lamont, N. 66
Länder 1, 2, 9–11, 15, 17, 22, 27, 33–43, 46, 70, 79–83, 93, 106, 112, 113, 124, 125, 131, 132, 134, 135
Lubbers, R. 60–3, 86
Luxembourg 61, 86
Luxembourg Compromise 55, 64, 85

Maastricht Treaty on European Union (TEU) 1–3, 8, 10–12, 14, 16, 26, 31, 33, 34, 40–6, 54, 57, 58, 61–3, 66, 67, 76–9, 81–9, 92–9, 102, 115, 125, 129–32, 134, 135
Major, J. 6, 11, 32, 66–8, 85, 87–9, 102, 119, 126, 128, 129, 133
Mandelson, P. 32
Mitterrand, F. 1, 56, 59, 61, 64, 65, 71, 84, 99, 115
Mölln 62
Monnet, J. 1

Index

Multilateralism 7, 10, 25, 30, 52, 54, 60, 77, 114, 117, 126, 127, 129, 134, 135

NATO 7, 29, 57, 60, 62, 64, 89, 126, 128
Netherlands 53, 60–4, 72, 73, 86, 87, 101, 102, 114, 116, 118, 119, 130, 133, 134
Neue Mitte 69, 70
Nölling, W. 97
North Rhine-Westphalia 36, 38

Oder–Neisse Frontier 61

Patten, C. 66
PDS 95, 98
Ploetz, H-F. 68
Poland 38, 104, 113, 116, 117

Qualified Majority Voting (QMV) 53, 56, 64, 77, 79, 80, 83, 84, 86, 89, 129

Republikaner 95
Rhineland Palatinate 81
Ridley, N. 4, 65

Saarland 36
Sauzay, B. 59
Saxony 27, 38, 96, 98, 112
Schachtschneider, K. 97
Scharping, R. 95
Schäuble, W. 32, 33
Schäuble–Lamers Paper 29, 33, 80, 95, 116
Schlesinger, H. 67
Schlüter, P. 94
Schmidt, H. 12, 53, 56
Schröder, G. 3, 7, 8, 10, 12, 18, 24, 26, 27, 54, 58–60, 68–71, 73, 95, 101, 106, 109–11, 117–19, 127, 129, 132, 133

Schuman Plan 1, 55
Selbsteinbindung 1, 3
Simon, D. 88
Single European Act (SEA) 10, 12, 14, 26, 40, 53, 56, 64, 124
Single Market 8, 10, 112, 113, 127
Slovenia 6, 61, 104
Social Chapter 6, 66, 67, 77, 87, 88
Socialist International 31
Solange I Judgment 44–6
Solange II Judgment 44, 46
Spain 70, 110
SPD 8, 10, 26, 29–31, 33, 58, 69, 70, 80–2, 95, 96, 98, 109
Spiegel, Der 79
Spöri, D. 95
St Malo Declaration 58
Stability Pact 63, 85, 86, 94, 95, 100, 101, 134
Stoiber, E. 37, 38, 80, 93, 94, 98, 108
Strauss-Kahn, D. 58, 101
Structural Funding 38, 39, 76, 80, 107, 108, 112
Sweden 69, 78

Tebbitt, N. 67
Thatcher, M. 1, 4, 6, 14, 31, 61, 64–7, 108, 119
Third Way 6, 101
Tietmeyer, H. 97
Trichet, J. 100
Trittin, J. 26
Turkey 12
Two-Plus-Four Conference 2, 126

UK–German Relations 54, 55, 64–70, 73, 87–89, 101, 102, 118–120, 128, 129
United Kingdom 2–8, 10–14, 16, 17, 28, 29, 31, 32, 53, 55–8, 60, 63–73, 76–8, 83–9, 95, 101, 102, 108–11, 114, 118–20, 126, 129, 130, 132, 133

USA 2, 5–7, 57, 65
USSR 2

Verheugen, G. 111
Voigt, K. 33
Volkswagen 38, 112

Waigel, T. 29, 94, 98, 108
Walther, G. 37, 82
Weimar Triangle 116, 117
Western European Union (WEU) 62, 77, 89
Wilson, H. 6

EU authorised representative for GPSR:
Easy Access System Europe, Mustamäe tee 50,
10621 Tallinn, Estonia
gpsr.requests@easproject.com

www.ingramcontent.com/pod-product-compliance
Ingram Content Group UK Ltd.
Pitfield, Milton Keynes, MK11 3LW, UK
UKHW021841140426
5217IPUK00022B/1544